Instant Vegas® 5

Instant Vegas® 5

Douglas Spotted Eagle & Jeffrey P. Fisher

San Francisco, CA

Published by CMP Books
an imprint of CMP Media LLC
600 Harrison Street, 6th Floor, San Francisco, CA 94107 USA
Tel: 415-947-6615; Fax: 415-947-6015
www.cmpbooks.com
email: books@cmp.com

Vegas® is a registered trademark of Sony Pictures Digital Inc. or its affiliates in the United States and other countries. Throughout this book Movie Studio refers to Sony® Screenblast® Movie Studio™. Designations used by companies to distinguish their products are often claimed as trademarks. In all instances where CMP is aware of a trademark claim, the product name appears in initial capital letters, in all capital letters, or in accordance with the vendor's capitalization preference. Readers should contact the appropriate companies for more complete information on trademarks and trademark registrations. All trademarks and registered trademarks in this book are the property of their respective holders.

The programs in this book are presented for instructional value. The programs have been carefully tested, but are not guaranteed for any particular purpose. The publisher does not offer any warranties and does not guarantee the accuracy, adequacy, or completeness of any information herein and is not responsible for any errors or omissions. The publisher assumes no liability for damages resulting from the use of the information in this book or for any infringement of the intellectual property rights of third parties that would result from the use of this information.

Distributed in the U.S. by:
Publishers Group West
1700 Fourth Street
Berkeley, CA 94710
1-800-788-3123

Distributed in Canada by:
Jaguar Book Group
100 Armstrong Avenue
Georgetown, Ontario M6K 3E7 Canada
905-877-4483

For individual orders and for information on special discounts for quantity orders, please contact:
CMP Books Distribution Center, 6600 Silacci Way, Gilroy, CA 95020
email: cmp@rushorder.com; Web: www.cmpbooks.com

ISBN: 1-57820-260-4

Dedication

For Douglas & Mannie: Thanks for all your support of my work.

—Jeffrey P. Fisher

For Jeffrey, Linda, Mannie, and the Vegas users who have made the Vegas books possible. Without you, we could not write.

—Douglas Spotted Eagle

Contents

Foreword

Douglas Spotted Eagle, aka Spot, and Jeffrey P. Fisher have been power users and instructors of Sony Media Software products since the earliest days of the products' existence. Both Spot and Jeffrey are visible leaders in the Vegas®, ACID®, and Sound Forge® software online communities. They continue to support the endeavors of new and experienced users alike, offering their expertise as Internet forum hosts, presenters on instructional DVDs, and authors of books like this one. Sony Media Software is pleased to have such talented producers creating training materials for our customers. If you have an interest in learning about the Vegas 5 program, this book will be an invaluable resource, helping you find out about the most important features in an instant. Enjoy!

Dave Chaimson

Vice President, Sony Media Software

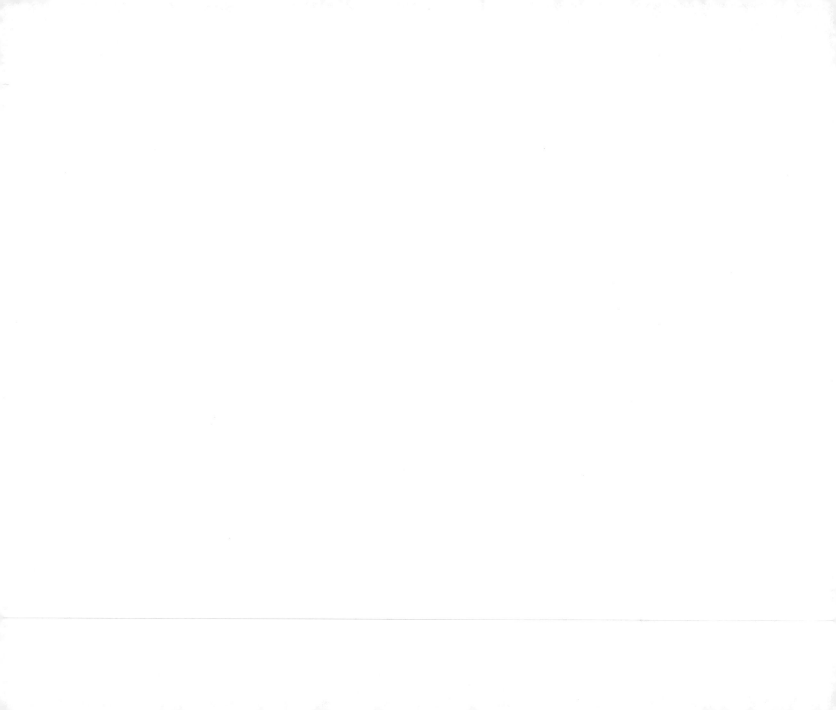

Acknowledgments

Jeffrey and Douglas would additionally like to thank:

Brad Reinke, Curtis Palmer, Dave Chaimson, Dave Hill, Richard Kim, Leigh Herman, Rick Hoefling, and all the other great folks at Sony Pictures Digital and Sony Broadcast for their support of the VASST series, Phil, Julie, Bob, Wanda, and the folks at Artbeats, Steve Pitzel and the gang at Intel, the iZotope team, the folks at WAVES, all the ACID gang, Michael at Pixelan, Aaron at Zenote, Satish Kumar, John Rofrano, (Johnny Roy) Lawrence Lim, Cindy Sheng, and the folks at New Magic Australia. Thanks to Mike Chenoweth, Mitch Richardson, Wes Howell, Mark Dileo, and the other VASST folks. Thank you to the folks at Digital Juice and Michelle at Serious Magic. Paul Temme, Dorothy Cox, thank you for seeing the VASST vision. Finally, a thanks to you, the reader. We hope to see you at one of our live training sessions.

We take responsibility for all content of this book. Any errors are indications of the temporary insanity that accompanies too much time in front of a flat screen. If you like the book, write us or the publisher and let us know. If you don't like the book, write to your congressman or favorite charity.

Jeffrey Fisher

Douglas Spotted Eagle (Spot)

All examples used in this book are courtesy of ARTBEATS. Thanks Phil, Julie, Bob, and all the other dedicated ARTBEATS folks. Visit   for a view of their astonishing libraries ranging from DV to High Definition.

Artbeats stock footage used in this book:

Chicago Aerials

Business Executives

Business World

Family Life

Mixed Cuts 2

Objects 360

Recreation and Leisure

Sports Metaphors

Starter Kit

Ultra Motion

Exceptions:

Lower-third graphic, Motion back, and "Lincoln" stills courtesy of Digital Juice

Turtle footage, newborn still, and VHS example from JPF's personal collection

Additional images are from DSE's personal collection

Introduction

Sony Vegas 5 is a powerful non-linear editor (NLE) and digital audio workstation (DAW) for audio-visual content destined for the Web, Powerpoint, CDs, CD-ROM, and/or DVDs. The software has extensive audio tools that are fully integrated with the video portion meaning your soundtracks can be as ear-popping as your visuals are eye-popping.

This book isn't intended as the definitive resource on this feature-packed program. Rather, our goal is to provide solutions to the most used features to get you up and running fasst and to provide quick refreshers when you're stumped about how to meet a goal. We also want to make you more comfortable with the software and push you to experiment with its tools to realize the vision you have for your own work.

You hold in your hands a highly visual guide with hundreds of screenshots that show you step-by-step how to use Vegas. The text is minimal, expounding with detail only when necessary. We suggest you have the Vegas software open as you work through the chapters. Try out the ideas we suggest, and discover your own unique ways of using the program. VEG files related to projects found in this book may be downloaded from the VASST website.

Whether you're new to Vegas or a seasoned user, we know you'll find this book helpful. Vegas is actually more powerful than it may seem on the surface. What's especially nice is as your skills grow, you'll continue to discover new features and new ways to apply them to your projects.

Other valuable tools include the burgeoning knowledge base for Vegas at Sundance Media Group/website (www.vasst.com) and the forums on Digital Media Net (www.dmnforums.com). On the VASST site you'll find dozens of VEG files, automation scripts, tutorials, and more. The VEG files are especially helpful as they let you get into the mind of other users and see how to get specific looks for your work. The DMN forums are like having dozens of experts ready to help you at a moment's notice. Check 'em out!

Both of us have been using Vegas since its inception as an audio-only program. We've used it for audio projects, music production, and, of course, videos. We've looked at and used many of the other NLEs available but always consider Vegas the best tool available today. Why? It's just plain fast, easy to learn, flexible, powerful, and stable (crashes are rare, if ever).

Jeffrey teaches the program at the College of Du-Page in Illinois and appreciates how fast students catch on. They edit faster, focusing on content, without having to learn every little button or wade through endless dialog boxes to accomplish the most mundane tasks.

Douglas has not only earned Grammy and Emmy awards with Vegas, he also has trained users from Ford Motor Company, the US Treasury, and many television station editors including editors from NBC's regional headquarters. With contributions to major motion pictures, television soundtracks, and winning several film festivals with his video productions, he uses Vegas as his primary editing tool because it allows him speed with extreme control and quality output.

His favorite comment about Vegas? "Vegas is the inspirational conduit from what you see in your mind's eye to what you see on the television screen."

Put simple: Vegas doesn't get in the way of your creativity. If that's what you want with your NLE software, read on.

A Note about Sony Movie Studio

Sony Movie Studio is what you might call "Vegas Lite." Just because it isn't listed as a "professional" application, consider that Vegas Movie Studio does more than any high end professional software application did five years ago, said professional applications costing tens of thousands of dollars. Vegas Movie Studio has many of the same features as its big brother, but is limited to only three audio and video tracks (Vegas is unlimited in the number of audio/video tracks you can create). Many of the tips, tricks, and techniques in these pages apply to Sony Movie Studio. Where they differ, we've noted in the text. Sony Movie Studio is an inexpensive --

yet powerful -- way to get your feet wet in the NLE world. You can put together some amazing videos with the program. As your skills grow, and your hunger for more possibilities deepens, Sony offers a clear upgrade path to the fully professional Vegas software. After reading what you can't do with Movie Studio (but can with Vegas), we know many of you will want to take that route. Best of all, project files created with Sony Movie Studio will open in Vegas (the opposite is not true, though). So, if you find your masterpiece started in Vegas Movie Studio isn't quite as polished and fancy enough, you won't have to start your project from scratch because Vegas will pick right up from where Vegas Movie Studio leaves off.

Who this Book Is For

This book is for all users of Vegas, beginner to advanced editors and creative types. Beginners will appreciate the no-fluff approach to intelligent use of Vegas, while those with more experience with Vegas will appreciate the projects and creative projects.

This book is written simply, to fulfill the needs of a broad range of ages, lifestyles, and creative abilities.

This book is for you.

Chapter 1

Hardware, Add-ons, and Installation

Vegas requires some specific PC hardware to run optimally. Though you may be able to get by with less, we don't recommend it. Here are the details to get you up and running fast with minimum fuss or muss. Also, we've included some additional hardware and software, though not required by Vegas, that can make using the program a better experience.

What's in the Box?

Vegas 5 and Vegas Movie Studio do not require any special hardware to work correctly. You just need to invest in a fairly robust computer system, but not expensive add-ons (unlike some other NLEs). According to Sony, Vegas 5 requires these minimum specs.

- Microsoft® Windows® 2000 or XP

- 500MHz processor

- 60MB hard-disk space for program installation

- 128MB RAM

- OHCI-compatible i.LINK® connector*/ IEEE-1394DV card (for DV capture and print-to-tape)

- Windows-compatible sound card

- CD-ROM drive

- Supported CD Recordable drive (for CD burning only)

- Supported DVD Recordable drive (for DVD burning only)

- Microsoft DirectX® 8 or later

- Microsoft .NET Framework 1.1

- Internet Explorer 5.0 or later

Note the word *minimum* above. Yeah, you could run the program successfully within these guidelines, but you'll be a happier camper if you exceed these numbers in a few critical areas. It's kinda like saying you could swat a fly with a pencil. More is better.

Use a faster processor. Vegas does take advantage of hyperthreading technology, so a fast 2.5MHz or higher hyperthreading Intel Pentium 4 is a terrific choice. Vegas works well with AMD processors of the FX or higher variety.

Get more RAM. We suggest 1GB (one gigabyte) as the optimum amount for Vegas 5. You'll generally experience smoother playback from the Timeline and the ability to apply more effects (audio and video) without glitching. Vegas doesn't need any special hardware to run, so judicious use of RAM gives it some of its magic.

Multiple hard drives. Working in DV demands some heavy drive space. One second of DV chews up about 3.5MB of space; an hour swallows 13GB of drive space. Put the Windows OS and your programs on the C drive and get a second hard drive for storing your media. Be sure to format any drives you use as NTFS (*not* Fat 32).

One particular device we recommend is the ADS Pyro 1394/USB2.0 Drive Kits (www.adstech.com). You put the hard drives of your choice into these data tanks. You can daisy-chain several of them for affordable, portable, high-capacity storage.

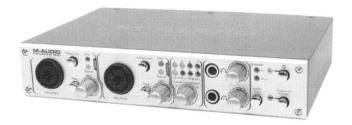

Use a better sound card. The internal card that shipped with your computer just won't cut it for professional video work. If you plan to record narration or track music, then upgrade your sound card. Planning to mix 5.1 surround sound? You'll need a card that supports six output channels.

Boys and Their Toys

We'd also like to mention some other optional gear you may wish to add to your Vegas workflow.

Bella Vegas keyboard (www.bella-usa.com). This custom keyboard includes Vegas commands printed on the keys and an integrated jog/shuttle wheel. This is one of Douglas' favorite tools for Vegas.

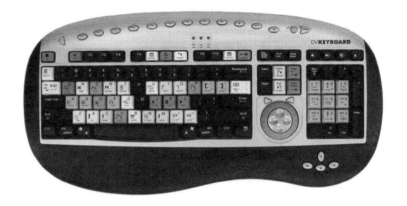

Vegas Custom keyboard from WorldTech Devices, Inc. (www.worldtechdevices.com). This USB keyboard also has over 130 Vegas shortcut commands laser-etched onto it.

Contour Design ShuttlePRO V2 (www.contourdesign.com). The mouse works. Keyboard shortcuts help. Scripting automates. Wouldn't it be great to have a jog/shuttle wheel and button access to your most-used tasks? And at the same time give your left hand something to do? Enter the Contour Design ShuttlePRO V2.

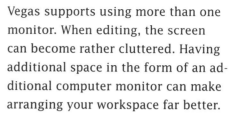

Vegas supports using more than one monitor. When editing, the screen can become rather cluttered. Having additional space in the form of an additional computer monitor can make arranging your workspace far better.

Is your work destined to play on TV? Don't make critical judgments without seeing your work on a real TV. One powerful feature of Vegas is its ability to preview on an external monitor via the FireWire port. Of course, you'll need something to convert the FireWire to analog video. Get a DV-to-analog converter such as the ADS Pyro A/V link (www.adstech.com) or the Canopus ADVC-100 (www.canopus.com) and a Sony broadcast monitor.

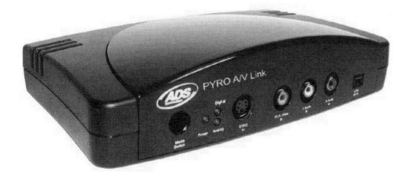

Cheapo computer speakers are not accurate enough for critical audio work. If the speakers are made of plastic, they won't cut it. Invest in quality speakers that come from music or video equipment suppliers. M-Audio, Mackie, Event, and Tannoy all make solid products. Choose self-powered speakers, often called active monitors.

Surround sound requires five full-range, matched speakers (stereo L/R, surround L/R, and center) and a low-frequency enhancement speaker (LFE).

Speaker placement is critical for correct monitoring. With stereo, your head and the two speakers should form an equilateral triangle (30° from center, 60° angle). Keep the tweeters at ear level with no obstructions. Placing the speakers in the free field away from a wall is better than near a boundary. Use isolator pads to get a more accurate sound.

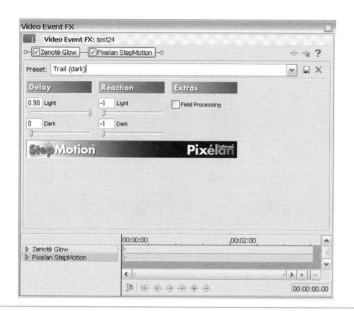

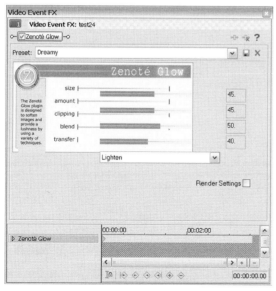

Looking Good

Though Vegas includes many powerful video effects, there are a few additional third-party effects you may want to consider.

Included with Vegas 5 is Boris Graffiti Ltd. (www.borisfx.com), a limited version of the popular Boris titling tool. Install this to get a feel for the additional titling power this brings to your productions.

Another in-the-Vegas-box plug-in is Red Giant's Magic Bullet Movie Looks (www.redgiantsoftware.com).

The Pixelan SpiceMaster 2 and Spice-Filters (www.pixelan.com) were the first third-party plug-ins available for Vegas. For organic, flowing transitions and effects, SpiceMaster 2 can't be beat. The SpiceFilters also give you some unique looks that must be seen to be believed.

Though Vegas Movie Studio ships with many video filters, it does not support these or any other third-party plug-ins.

Zenote (www.zenote.com) provides a unique collection of Vegas filters that offer some unique and much-sought-after effects. Douglas uses these to get a film-like look from video.

Satish Kumar (www.debugmode.com) has been providing plug-ins for Vegas for several years now. His latest, Wax, includes 3D effects, particles, and more.

VASST Ultimate S is a new scripting tool with major time-saving functions including auto slide shows with Pan/Crop movements.

Excalibur and Neon (found at www.vegastoolsandtraining.com) are two script-based plug-ins that speed up editing tremendously. Panopticum (www.panopticum.com) is yet another plug-in series for Vegas that while slow to render, provides some amazing creative options.

Movie Studio Users: Though Vegas Movie Studio ships with many video filters, it does not support these or any other third-party plug-ins.

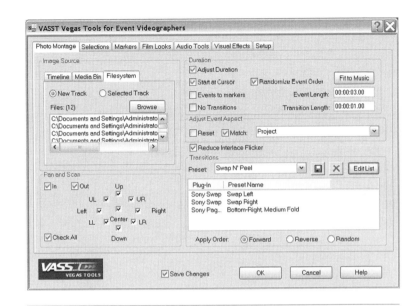

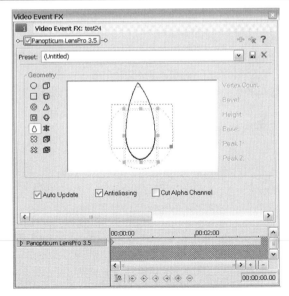

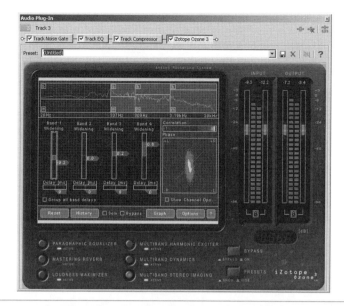

Sounding Better

Because of its strong roots in audio, Vegas includes several useful audio effects. It also supports DirectX (DX) plug-ins, which opens up the program to dozens of third-party entries. For a complete list of audio-based plug-ins, check out the DirectXFiles (at www. directxfiles.com).

Both Douglas and Jeffrey consider Izotope Ozone 3 (www.izotope.com) a desert-island plug-in. This multi-effects processor is well suited to master music and audio for video.

Speaking of Sony Sound Forge, this mono- and two-track editor complements Vegas' audio functions quite well. It's a jam-packed program with plenty of depth. Check out Jeffrey's *Instant Sound Forge* book from VASST/ CMP Books or his five-hour DVD from VASST for more details.

Movie Studio Users: Though Vegas Movie Studio includes several audio effects, it does not support these or any other DirectX plug-ins.

Up and Running

Drop the Vegas or Vegas Movie Studio disc in your CD-ROM drive and follow the instructions. If you downloaded the program, double-click the file and follow the prompts.

After the install, launch the program. For Vegas, enter your serial number and then three choices for registration display. If you're connected to the Internet, choose register online. If you prefer to register on another computer, that requires you to copy a file to a floppy and take it to a computer with Internet access. You'll be sent an activation code via e-mail that unlocks the software. Or you may register over the phone.

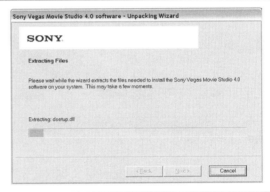

Movie Studio Users: To register Vegas Movie Studio, enter your serial number. Next indicate whether you want to register with contact information or not. If connected to the Internet, the software will then register, and you can begin using it.

Movie Studio Users: Here's a hidden gem. If your computer does not have Internet access and you wish to register Vegas, click register without contact information. The program tries to connect to the web and fails. This time click Cancel, and you're given the option to register over the telephone.

One Click and You're Done

Vegas supports the Microsoft .NET framework, which allows you to run Java and Visual Basic mini-applets within the software. These scripts, as they are called, can automate many routines within Vegas.

To run scripts in Vegas 5, you need the latest version of Microsoft .NET installed. It's available free from Microsoft (www.microsoft.com) or through Windows update. It's also included on the Vegas installation disc.

Movie Studio Users: Vegas Movie Studio does not support scripting.

Some scripts written for Vegas 4 may not run properly in Vegas 5. If this happens, navigate to the script file, right-click it, then choose Edit. In the editor (usually just Windows Notepad), search the script for any reference to "SonicFoundry. Vegas" and change it to "Sony.Vegas." This line will typically be near the top of the script file. Save the file. (Sony acquired Vegas from Sonic Foundry in July 2003).

Chapter 2

It's Vegas, Baby

Let's take a closer look at these powerful programs, tour their interfaces, and customize them to the way you work.

The Nickel Tour

Vegas and Vegas Movie Studio look a little different compared to other NLEs. The Timeline dominates the computer screen and is where you'll be doing most of your editing work. There is only one video monitor, which does double duty as both a way to preview individual files and the project as a whole.

Access the various menus by clicking the words along the screen top. Below these menus is the toolbar providing one-click access to many functions. Directly under the toolbar on the left is the time display. Under this, along the left of the screen is the track list. Adjacent to the track list is the Timeline. Above the Timeline is the time ruler. Along the bottom, under the Timeline, is the window docking area. The default layout in both Vegas and Vegas positions a tabbed grouping of most-used functions on the left, the Master volume fader in the center, and the video preview window to the far right.

Buzzword Alert: Events

Vegas will not accept Avid-captured files, as Avid's video format doesn't always play nicely with other NLEs.

Vegas and Vegas Movie Studio call every element added to the Timeline an event. Events can be video files, still pictures, generated media, or audio tracks. Only video events can reside on video tracks; likewise for audio. Most important, both programs are format-agnostic, which means you can mix and match supported file types on a track. It's possible to crossfade a monaural MP3 into a stereo CD track and preview this in real-time without any problems. You can go from still to motion video and back again without any issues to concern you either.

Menus

Along the top of the screen are typical menus: File, Edit, View, Insert, Tools, Options, and Help. Click a menu to reveal the choices associated with it. Menu selections in this book are separated by a greater-than sign (>). For example, File>Save As means to click the File menu, navigate to and then click Save As.

Menu names indicate primary functions.

- File—provides access to importing, exporting and saving files.

- Edit—shows functions related to editing on the Timeline.

- View—turns on and off what displays on your screen. If you can't find something, chances are you've turned it off accidentally. Use the view menu (or learn the keyboard shortcuts) to recall missing elements.

- Insert—adds tracks, buses, generated media, and more.

- Tools—provides a variety of helpful utilities.

- Options—turns on and off many functions.

- Help—accesses program help and other information.

You can access most menu functions by right-clicking with the mouse, too. For example, right-clicking a video event on the Timeline displays Edit menu functions (and a few other helpful tools).

Toolbar

The toolbar is directly under the menu choices and spans the entire workspace. Many of these buttons duplicate menu operations. Hover the mouse over a tool to display a tooltip indicating its function.

In Vegas 5, the default toolbar contains:

- New—starts a new project.

- Open—opens a previously saved project.

- Save—saves the current project.

- Project Properties—displays the Project Properties dialog box (Alt+Enter is the shortcut).

- Cut—removes the current selection to the clipboard (for temporary data storage).

- Copy—copies the current selection to the clipboard.

- Paste—inserts the clipboard contents at the cursor position.

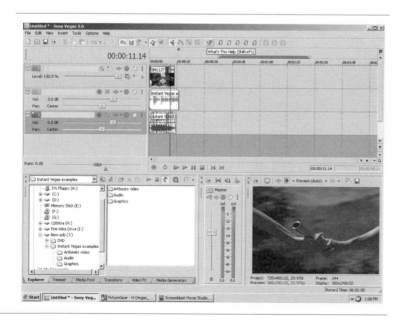

- Undo—removes the previous operation. Click the arrow next to the undo button to drop down the list of operations. You can undo a series this way.

- Redo—performs the last operation again. Click the arrow next to the redo button for the list.

- Enable snapping—turns on snapping. Click the Options menu to choose which elements to snap to, including Quantize to Frames, Snap to Grid, or Snap to Markers. Hold Shift while moving an event to temporarily override this setting. F8 toggles snapping on and off.

- Automatic Crossfades—causes overlapping events to crossfade (the first event fades out, while the second event fades in).

- Auto Ripple—forces ripple mode on while editing. There are different ripple modes available, which are discussed later in the book.

- Lock Envelopes to Events—keeps envelopes that control certain parameters attached to their events. When moving the event, the associated envelope moves, too.

- Ignore Event Grouping—enables defined groups, including video with its associated audio, to be moved independently.

- Normal Edit Tool—used for most editing tasks.

- Envelope Edit Tool—defines and edits envelopes.

- Selection Edit Tool—allows selection of multiple events. The standard Windows command of Ctrl+click allows selection of multiple events, too.

- Zoom Edit Tool—used for zooming. There are other zoom buttons available and discussed below.

- What's This Help—displays help text when you click it and point to something else.

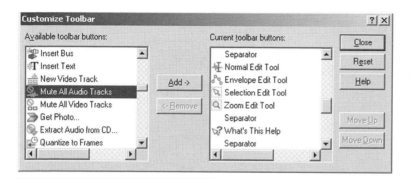

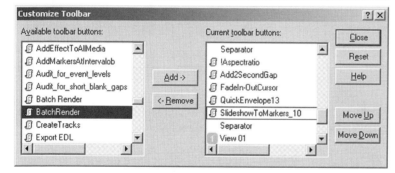

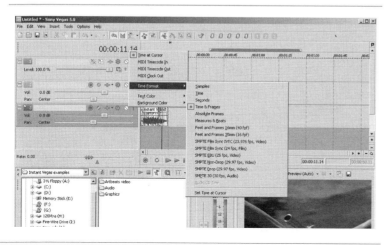

Both Vegas and Vegas Movie Studio let you customize the toolbar to your liking. Click Options>Customize Toolbar.

The left side of the dialog box shows the available buttons; the right side shows the buttons currently in use.

Scroll through the list to find a button. Position where you want to place the button in the right pane and click Add. The button appears on the toolbar. For Vegas users, add automation scripts to the toolbar for one-click access.

Left-click the time ruler, and the cursor changes into a hand. Drag it to quickly scroll through your project.

Time Display and Time Ruler

The time display and time ruler across the top of the Timeline work together. Right-click the time display and navigate to Time Format for available choices. Note that the ruler changes, too.

Right-click the time ruler itself for access to the same choices. Or choose Options>Ruler Format instead.

Movie Studio Users: The time display and ruler are fixed at time and frames.

Track List

Using colors is one way to organize your project. For example, you may have several drum tracks in a music project. Changing them to be all one color makes finding and working with them easier.

Vegas supports unlimited audio and video tracks. As mentioned above, only video can reside on a video track and only audio on an audio track. However, you can mix and match supported file types on an appropriate track, though.

To move a track, click its number and drag it up or down to a new position.

To change the track color, right-click the track number and navigate to Track Display Color and choose from the available options.

Movie Studio Users: You are limited to three each of video and audio tracks, and their positions are fixed.

Vegas track names are blank. Vegas Movie Studio provides a default name. To change the scribble strip in either program, double-click it and type in a new name. Or right-click and choose Rename from the menu and then type.

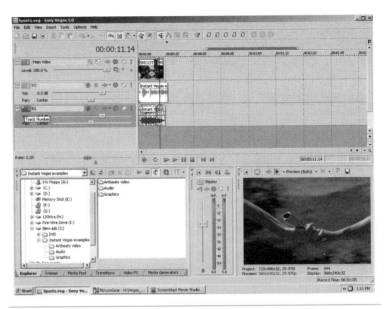

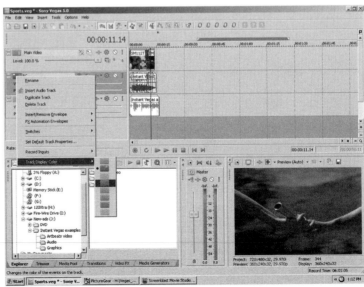

There are several ways to insert a video or audio track:

- Right-click the empty Timeline and choose Insert Audio Track or Insert Video Track.

- Use the keyboard shortcuts: Ctrl+Q for an audio track or Ctrl+Shift+Q for a video track.

- Click the Insert menu and choose either Audio Track or Video Track.

- Drag an audio or video file from the Explorer to an empty space on the Timeline and release.

Video Tracks

Video tracks follow a top-down hierarchy, meaning that the top track obscures any tracks below it. This can be changed through opacity, compositing modes, picture-in-picture effects, and alpha (transparent) channels, such as a title. There will be additional detail on these topics later in the book.

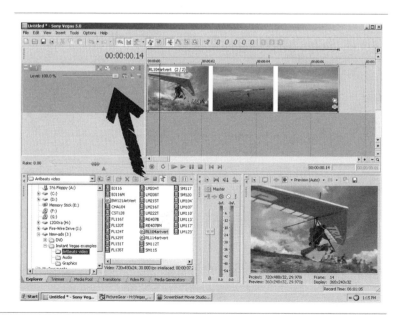

Each video track header contains several buttons and a single slider.

Multiple tracks (audio and video) can be muted or soloed at one time. Select a track or tracks and press X to toggle solo on and off and Z to toggle mute on and off.

- Bypass motion blur—turns off motion blur added at the project level for every event on the track.

- Track motion—accesses the track motion dialog for 2D and 3D picture-in-picture effects.

- Track FX—applies video effects or filters to every event on the track.

- Automation Settings—accesses automation controls for the track.

- Mute—turns off the track.

- Solo—turns off all other tracks, leaving this track on.

- Level (Opacity)—controls the opacity of all events in the track. 100 percent is fully opaque, while 0 percent is fully transparent.

- Compositing mode—displays a menu of compositing choices, including 3D, new to Vegas 5.

- Make Compositing Parent—turns the track into a compositing parent.

- Make Compositing Child—makes the track a compositing child.

Movie Studio Users: Video tracks only have mute and solo buttons.

Audio Tracks

Both programs treat each audio track as stereo, which means you don't have to tie up two tracks for one stereo file. If the audio track is mono, it's treated as dual mono (equal energy in both channels). Right-click an audio event and choose Channels from the menu for additional control over how Vegas handles the stereo (or mono) content.

Each audio track header contains buttons and two sliders.

- Arm for Record—selects the track for recording.

- Invert Track Phase—switches the phase of the audio by 180 degrees.

- Audio Track FX—accesses the audio plug-in dialog and applies chosen effects to all events on the track.

- Automation Settings—accesses the track's automation controls.

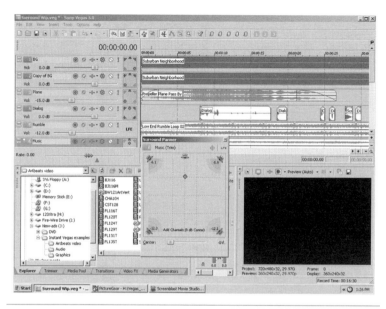

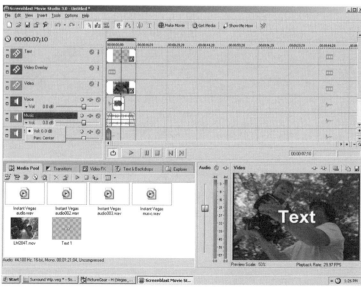

- Mute—turns off the track.

- Solo—turns off all other tracks, leaving this track on.

- Vol: (Volume)—controls the overall level of the track.

- Pan—controls the stereo positioning of the track.

For surround-sound (5.1) projects, Vegas replaces the Pan slider with the Surround Sound Panner.

Movie Studio Users: Audio tracks only have Arm for Record, Audio Track FX, and Mute. The slider does double duty. Click the arrow to choose whether the slider affects volume or pan. There is also no support for surround sound.

Timeline

The Timeline holds all the audio and video events comprising your project. Use the horizontal scroll bar to move through the project and the vertical scroll bar to move through the tracks. Click and drag the far edges of the horizontal scroll bar to zoom in and out.

In the lower-right corner, the vertical + and – buttons control track height, and the horizontal + and – buttons control time zoom.

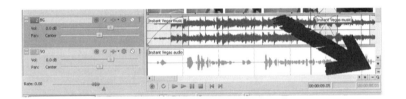

Click the magnifying glass. The cursor changes to a magnifying glass. Now click and drag a selection over your Timeline to zoom in to what you selected. This is a one-shot zoom tool. Switch to the zoom edit tool on the toolbar to stay in zoom mode.

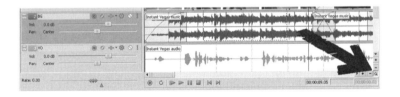

Directly below the Timeline are the transport controls.

- Record—click this or Ctrl+R to launch the record dialog box.

- Loop—plays the time selection continuously. The Q key toggles this feature on and off.

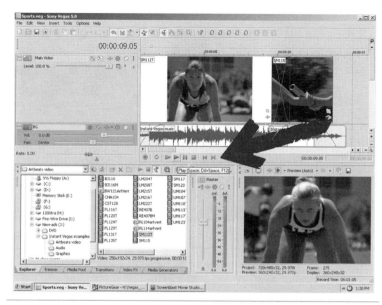

- Play from start—returns to the project's beginning and plays.

- Play—plays from the cursor's position forward. The spacebar duplicates this function.

- Pause—pauses playback at the current cursor position. The Enter key duplicates this function.

- Stop—stops playback and returns to the cursor start position. The spacebar and Esc duplicates this function.

- Go to start—rewinds to the beginning of the project. Ctrl+Home, and W are shortcuts.

- Go to end—fast-forwards to the project's end. Ctrl+End is the keyboard shortcut.

The scrub control tool is to the left of the transport controls and below the track list. Dragging the slider controls how slowly or quickly your project plays. Hover the mouse over the scrub control, and use the mouse wheel to control the slider instead.

Movie Studio Users: The scrubbing tool and JKL scrubbing are not available.

Timeline scrubbing is also available on the keyboard using the J, K, and L keys. Pressing J scrubs through your project in reverse, L scrubs forward, and K pauses. Repeatedly pressing the J and L keys speeds up the scrubbing. Holding down the K key while pressing either the J or L key starts the scrubbing at a slower rate.

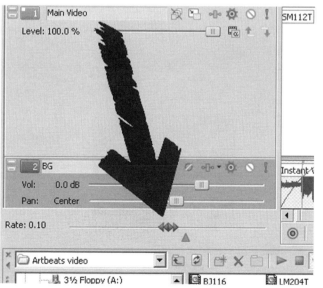

Window Docking Area

Along the bottom of the Vegas and Vegas screens is the window docking area. This customizable area (Vegas only) gives you access to a variety of tools and utilities. A series of tabs dominate the left side.

The Explorer doesn't automaticallly rescan your hard drive. If you perform some operation in another program, such as a graphics program, and save a file, it will not appear in the Vegas or Vegas Explorer unless you click the Refresh button. Refresh rescans the drive and updates the display.

Explorer—this duplicates the function of the standard Windows Explorer. Use it to navigate and organize your content across multiple drives. Select a file (audio, video, or still) and click the play button to preview it. Click stop button to stop previewing. The spacebar duplicates these function in Explorer, too. Click the Auto Preview button, and whenever you click a file, it automatically previews.

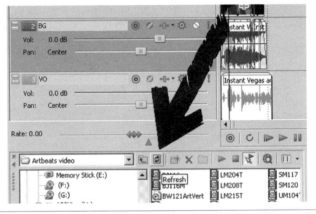

Trimmer—this tool allows you to work on sections of a longer file and add them to the project. It has its own transport controls and several other tools that speed up editing tasks.

Movie Studio Users: The Trimmer isn't supported.

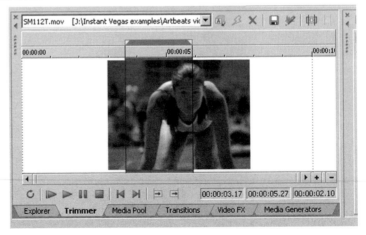

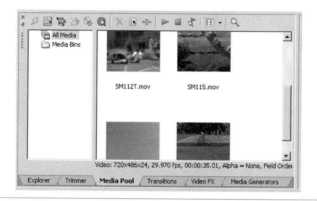

Media Pool—Vegas offers a handy way to organize your project content in one place. Set up multiple folders and arrange your media as needed. The Media Pool also provides access to the tools necessary to add content such as video capture, extracting CDs, and more. You can even add filters and effects in the Media Pool. Important: the media pool is a virtual organizational tool. It does *not* store or move media, only points to where the media resides on your computer.

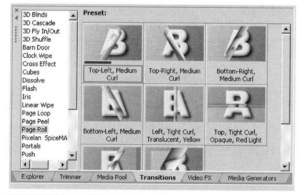

Transitions—displays the name of available video transitions on the left and animated thumbnails on the right. Click a thumbnail to see it animate. The A refers to the outgoing media and the B refers to the incoming media.

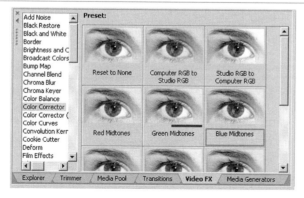

Video FX—displays available video effects on the left and thumbnails to the right. Click the thumbnail for an animated preview.

Media Generators—displays the available options to the left and thumbnails on the right.

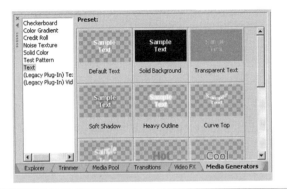

Master—this controls the main output level of the audio in your project. The sliders controlling output level can be locked or moved independently by clicking the lock at the bottom of the screen. The two meters represent the left and right channels comprising a stereo mix. The meter top is 0 (the loudest), while the other numbers are negatives (getting progressively softer).

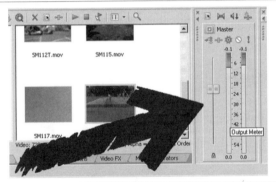

Preview—this window does double duty as it allows you to both preview individual files and your project as a whole.

Movie Studio Users: The Media Generators tab is called Text and Backdrops, the Master audio fader is called Audio, and the video preview is called Video.

If the audio level displays in red, the project exceeds 0 on the meters. This results in unwanted distortion. Reduce the levels until the level stays below 0 all the time.

If you are not seeing a tab, click the view menu. Anything currently displaying in the workspace has a check mark next its name. Click the name to add the check mark and the tool displays.

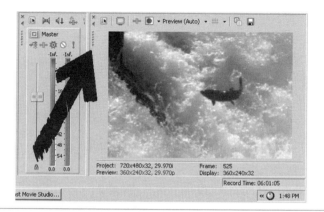

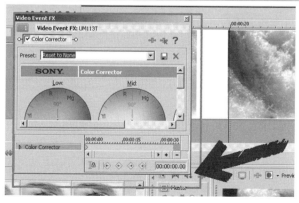

Customize Your Workspace

Vegas allows you to position windows and alter the workspace to fit your particular needs. There is even dual monitor support for more workspace flexibility. To move a window, click its handle (the six bumpy dots) and then drag the window into position.

You can float multiple windows or dock them.

To resize a window or dialog box, hover over the edge until the cursor changes to two arrows.

Click and drag to resize. Clicking and dragging a corner makes resizing faster. Click the arrows in the window docking area for one-click resizing.

Movie Studio Users: You can resize workspace and dialog box boundaries, but you can't customize the workspace as mentioned above.

- **F11 hides and shows the window docking area.**
- **Shift+F11 hides and shows the track list.**
- **Ctrl+F11 hides and shows both the window docking area and track list.**
- **Press ` (above the Tab key) to minimize all tracks and Ctrl+` to return tracks to their default height.**

Save and Recall Workspaces

Vegas 5 can save and recall up to 10 custom workspaces.

- Arrange the workspace to your liking.

- Press Ctrl+Alt+D and release.

- Press any keyboard number key, 1–0 (not the keypad) to store the workspace.

- Rearrange the workspace to a new configuration and repeat the steps.

To recall a workspace, press Alt+D, release, then press the keyboard number corresponding to the workspace you want to see.

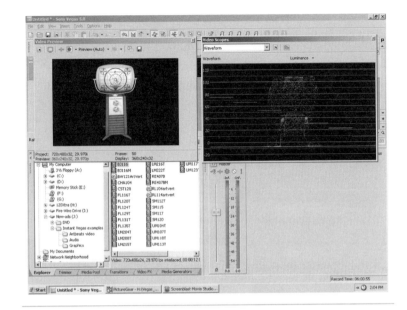

Keyboard Shortcuts

Learning keyboard shortcuts can greatly increase your editing efficiency. Many are standard Windows commands that work across all applications.

Here are some handy Vegas keyboard shortcuts you will want to remember.

- Ctrl+D selects the normal edit tool.

- Ctrl+ Home returns to the beginning of the Timeline (as does W). Home goes to the start of the currently displayed Timeline, and End goes to the end of the currently displayed Timeline. Ctrl+End goes to the end of the project.

- Spacebar toggles play and stop on the Timeline, returning the cursor to the start position.

- Enter pauses playback, leaving the cursor where it is.

- F12 toggles play and stop even if the Timeline doesn't have the focus.

- Shift+F12 (Or Shift+Spacebar) plays from the project start.

- Esc stops playback.

- Up arrow zooms in on the Timeline; down arrow zooms out.

- Left and right arrows move through the Timeline frame by frame.

- Backslash (\) centers the cursor in the Timeline.

- Ctrl+Up Arrow zooms in to the time selection.

- S splits an event or multiple selected events, the split point determined by cursor placement.

There are many other keyboard shortcuts, and we urge you to learn them. Click Help>Keyboard shortcuts.

The list displays by tasks. Try to learn a new shortcut every time you use Vegas, and you'll be amazed how much they speed up your workflow.

If you use either a Bella keyboard or a Contour Design ShuttlePro V2, assign your most-used shortcuts to the programmable buttons, too.

Adjusting Parameters

To adjust the sliders in various dialog boxes, click with your left mouse button and drag it for a coarse adjustment. For finer control over the settings, click *both* the left and right mouse buttons and drag the slider at the same time. Alternately, hold down the Ctrl key while clicking and dragging the slider. Click a slider and use the up and down arrow keys, too.

You can also enter values by typing them into the corresponding box.

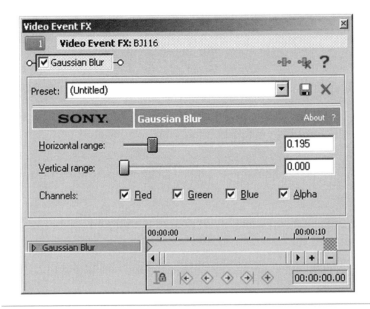

A Note About V5 Scripts

As mentioned earlier, Vegas has a sub-folder called Script Menu under Program Files>Sony>Vegas folder. We suggest that you move any scripts to this folder.

After you've put any scripts in this folder, launch Vegas 5 and click Tools>Scripting, then Rescan Script Menu Folder. All your scripts, including those shipped with Vegas 5, appear on the list.

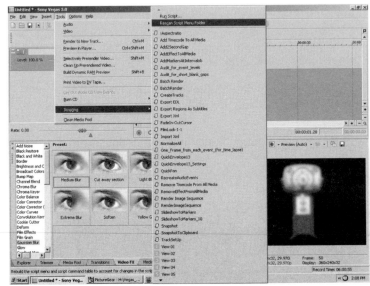

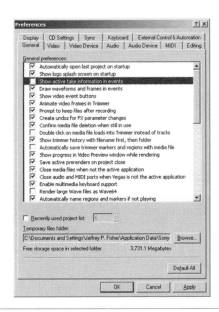

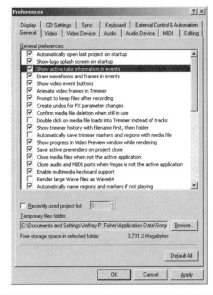

Of course, you can still use Options>Customize Toolbars to add scripts as buttons to the toolbar, too. See the instruction earlier in this chapter for details.

I Did It My Way

There are more customization options for using Vegas and Vegas. Click Options>Preferences to access them. Click a tab to see available options. Make any changes you deem appropriate. To save your settings, click OK when you are finished making changes to the software preferences.

General Tab

Put a check mark in "Show active take information in events." This displays the name and other information about events on the Timeline.

Make sure there is a checked box in the "Ignore third party DV codecs" and that there is *not* a checked box in "Use Microsoft DV codec."

Video Tab

Change the "Dynamic RAM Preview max (MB)" to the "Max available" amount indicated. This allows Vegas to use all your available RAM for previews.

Other preferences and software settings are discussed where appropriate later in this book.

Audio Tab

Change the "Normalize peak level (db)" to -0.3.

Audio Device

From the "Audio device type" drop-down box, choose the appropriate sound card. If you are using an internal sound card that shipped with your computer, the Microsoft Sound Mapper will suffice, but you may achieve better performance with the Windows Classic Wave Driver. If your sound card supports ASIO drivers, this will show up in the Audio device type drop-down. Use ASIO drivers if they're available.

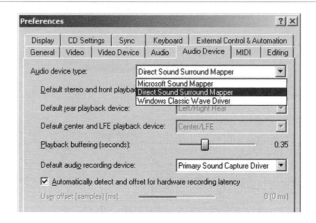

Chapter 3

Getting the Good Stuff In

Now it's time to discuss the NLE workflow and how to import the media you need for your project, organize it, and prepare to start editing.

Off to Workflow We Go

Before you can begin using these powerful software NLEs, it's helpful to understand the process, or workflow. There are three main steps: manage all the resources, bring them together into a coherent and appealing aural and visual experience, and output the finished project.

Step One: Manage Resources

Understanding how both audio and video flow through a project may be helpful. Click Help>Contents and Index or press F1, navigate to the Index tab and type "Signal." Double-click the Signal Flow Diagram choice that displays and choose either Signal Flow Diagram from the list for audio or Video Signal Flow Diagram for video.

- Gather the material you need (video, stills, graphics, etc.)
- Log your video footage by watching the video and making notes.
- Import the video clips into the computer.
- Import other media to the computer.
- Create or find other necessary material .

Step Two: Organize Resources into a Complete Video

- Arrange audio and video elements on the software Timeline.
- Transition between these elements.
- Add titles.
- Add music, sound effects, and mix the audio.

Step Three: Render the Final Video

- Print to tape, burn a DVD, stream a little stream, etc.

Project file notes

Both Vegas and Vegas Movie Studio use project files. Neither program stores media with its associated file (.VEG and .VF respectively). This means the media stays in place on your hard drives. The software only points to, or references the media.

NLE editing is also non-destructive. This means that all the work in your project file does not affect the actual media. It remains untouched in its original condition. Vegas and Vegas Movie Studio work with the media, applying effects in real time, but don't change the media permanently.

As a consequence, the project file must be rendered to apply all the project attributes—your hard work—to a finished file. This file is also separate from the original media.

Movie Studio Users: You may see references to "Video Factory" when using the program. That was its former name before Sony purchased the software from Sonic Foundry in July, 2003. It's also why the file extension is VF.

If you delete or move the media, the program tells you what's missing when you reopen the project file. You have options for locating the media and updating the project. Instruct Vegas to search for missing media in the pop-up dialog.

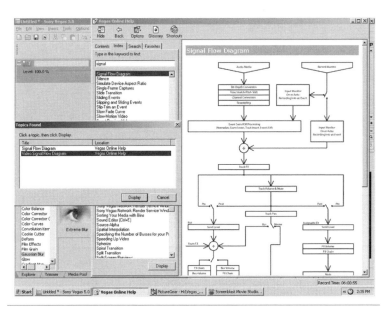

New Projects and Properties

Launch Vegas or Vegas Movie Studio. There may be an icon on your desktop, or point to the Windows Start menu>All Programs>Sony and continue to navigate to the program. Drag the desktop icon to the Windows taskbar to enable a taskbar shortcut to the application.

To start a new project, click File>New, click the New button on the toolbar, or use the keyboard shortcut Ctrl+N.

The Project Properties dialog box displays. There are several tabs from which to choose.

Video—displays the video options. We suggest that you choose a template from the drop-down box by clicking the arrow. The default, NTSC DV (720×480), 29.97fps, matches the video properties of Mini-DV camcorders. It's the best choice in this case. The PAL equivalent is the PAL DV (720×576, 25fps template.

Audio—shows the audio-related options. Again, sticking with the defaults is fine for most instances.

If you use multiple external drives, you may get these messages frequently depending on how drive letters get assigned. All your media may be on an F drive, but the next time you fire up the drive, it may be assigned drive letter G. Both Vegas and Vegas Movie Studio will be looking on F for your media. Quickly point to the media now on drive G and continue working.

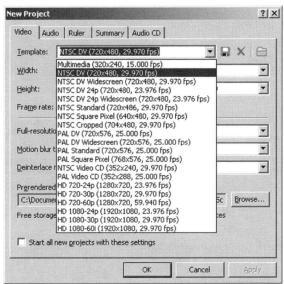

Vegas users would change the "Master bus mode" to 5.1 surround (click the arrow to display the drop-down list) if your project will be in surround.

Ruler—sets the time ruler properties along with the measures and beats (useful for music projects).

Summary—includes information about the project.

Audio CD—Vegas can burn Red Book-compliant CDs from the Timeline. Enter pertinent information here if your Vegas project is an audio CD. Note that you can start the disc with a track other than the first one on the Timeline.

Make sure you click OK to make any changes you made to the project properties apply. If you need to access the project properties again, click File>Properties or use the keyboard shortcut Alt+Enter.

You can also click the Project Audio Properties button or Project Video Properties button in the audio mixer and video preview windows respectively.

After creating a new file, it's a really good idea to name it by saving it. See below.

Beats per minute (on the Audio tab of the Project Properties dialog box) is the tempo that any imported ACID loops will match. Make sure you set this *before* adding ACID loops to your Vegas project.

After making changes to Project Properties, click the check box "Start all new projects with these settings" to preserve changes for all future new Vegas projects.

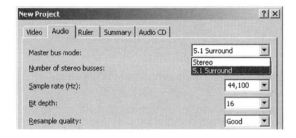

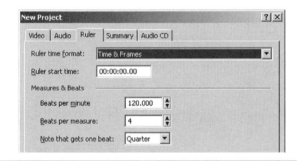

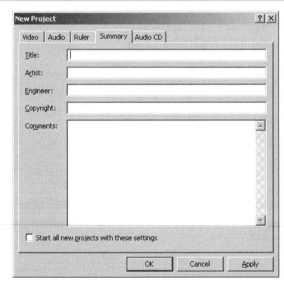

Open, Close, Save, Save As

To open an existing project, click File>Open, click the Open button on the toolbar, or use the keyboard shortcut Ctrl+O. Navigate to the file using the dialog box that displays and then click Open.

Alternately, use the Explorer to locate the project file and click, drag, and drop it on the Timeline to open the existing project.

To save a project, click File>Save, click the Save button on the toolbar, or use the keyboard shortcut Ctrl+S. Use the dialog box to name your project and also decide where it should reside on your computer.

Save As is useful for saving projects to new names. Click File>Save As to access the dialog. Since neither Vegas nor Vegas Movie Studio keep media with the project file, the file sizes are quite small. It can make real sense to save works in progress. This serves two purposes. One, you can experiment with different ideas and return to earlier versions. Two, you have a backup of your work should something happen to your original file.

Another terrific feature of the Save As dialog is for packaging projects. When you've finished a project, click File>Save As. Give your project a final name and navigate to the folder to hold it. Put a check in the box "Copy and trim media with project" and click Save.

The next dialog box gives you the option of copying whole or just trimmed media to the same location as the project file. Trimmed media are just the parts used in the project, not the entire files. This is terrific for getting everything together in one place on the hard drive. That makes backups or sharing projects with others a snap.

To Media Pool or not to Media Pool

The choice of using the Media Pool or not to organize your projects is up to you. Douglas sets up several bins and moves content into those bins. For example, he creates three main bins: Audio, Video, and Graphics. In Video, there is a stock footage bin, B-roll bin, and a bin for each interview, main section, or tape. In the Audio bins, there is an ACID loops bin, an MP3 bin, and a WAV bin. In the graphics bins, he creates a stock image bin, and a project pictures bin. This helps with logging for broadcast reports.

An asterisk (*) in the title bar (next to the file name) means there are unsaved changes in the current project. Make sure you save projects periodically.

We can't emphasize enough the importance of backups. Use the 2×2 rule: two copies in two different places (different hard drives or computers, CD, etc.) There are even free scripts to assist with this. (Vegas does save .bak files as backups if this is enabled in Options> Preferences.)

With the Media Pool open, right-click the Media Bins folder and choose Create New Bin from the pop-up menu.

Type a name for the bin and press Enter. Continue to create bins (and sub-bins) as needed.

You can populate your bins as you import media, capture video, and so forth. You can also drag and drop files from one bin to another. Remember that files are not physically moved when using the Media Pool as it is only a project-level, virtual organization tool. The files remain wherever they originally resided on your computer.

Jeffrey prefers to organize content on the hard drive first and rarely uses the Media Pool as an organizational tool. His approach is to create a single, top-level Project folder and put all the relevant Vegas files in it. Under this main folder he then creates a series of folders (video, graphics, audio, renders, and DVD) and several subfolders under each main category. He then moves media into appropriate folders as needed.

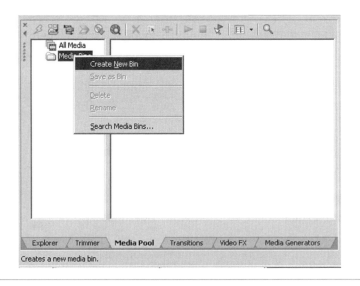

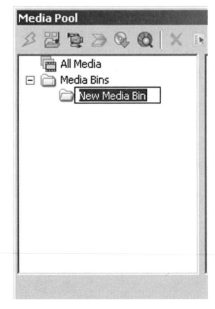

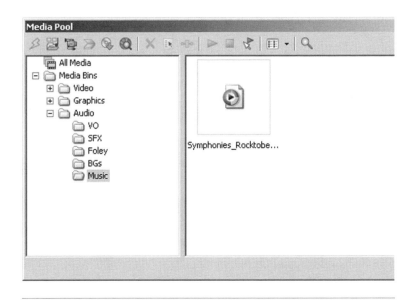

Video

- Interviews and tapes (one subfolder per tape)
- B-Roll
- Stock footage
- Backgrounds, animations, etc.

Graphics

- Still photographs
- Graphics and logos

Audio

- VO
- Foley
- Music
- Hard effects
- Backgrounds

Renders

- Pre-renders
- Segment and sequence renders
- Final renders (often in several formats, e.g. AVI, MPG, etc.)

DVD Project Files

- Authoring files
- Prepared projects (from Sony DVD-A)

Import Media

To add media to the Media Pool, have it open and then click the Import Media button or choose File>Import media.

Use the dialog box to navigate to the media and click Open.

Notice that the file is added to the media bin but not the project Timeline.

Change how files display in the Media Pool by clicking the Views button and making a selection.

It's important to have the correct bin in place—and selected—before importing media, otherwise the media may not be organized as intended.

If the files you are importing are on removable media, such as stock video footage on a CD-ROM, consider moving the files to a folder on the hard drive *before* importing the clips into the Media Pool. Otherwise, if you remove the CD, the files will be unavailable for your project.

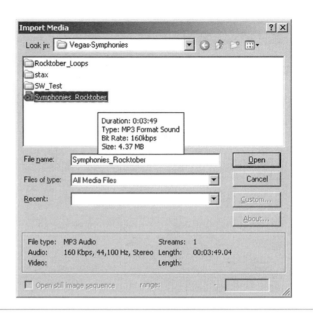

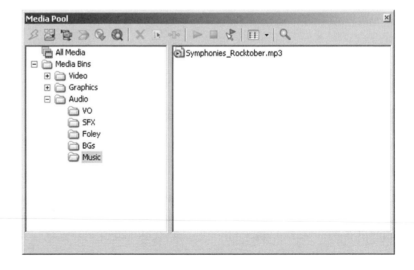

Capturing Video Workflow

There are several workflow approaches when capturing video.

Capture everything—with this approach, you capture entire tapes (usually as one long file). Then, use the Vegas Trimmer to slice and dice the video. Markers, regions, and subclips will help you organize the clips.

Automatic scene detection—this approach captures entire tapes with "Enable DV scene detection" turned on (it is by default). Instead of one long file, the software chops up the file based on scene changes (basically when the camcorder was stopped and started during shooting). Scene detection works only for DV devices.

Advanced capture—this technique means going through the tape manually and setting in- and out-points for the clips you want to use. After logging these selections, Vegas automatically captures the clips.

Movie Studio Users: Advanced capture mode is not offered.

Manual—with this method, watch the tape and capture clips manually as they play.

Live capture—Capturing video directly to the hard drive during shooting.

Logging

You must watch your footage carefully to see what you really have. If you are editing video that somebody else shot, this step is critical. This is called logging and can be done before, during, or after capture.

- Before lets you focus on the video and not worry about technical issues. Hook up the camcorder to a TV, curl up on the couch, watch, and take notes.

- During means watching, evaluating, and capturing at the same time. Coupled to advanced capture this approach can make for efficient capture sessions.

- After means getting the clips into the computer first and then logging the material. This is a fine approach for shorter projects. For longer projects where you'll be using much of what you shot, such as a training video, this can work, too. However, for a long documentary, where you shot 50 hours of tape, you may want to consider a hybrid of the before and during method, capturing only the footage you think you'll use.

Get the Hookup

Capturing from a DV camcorder requires an OHCI-compliant 1394 port on your computer. Called i.LINK® by Sony, or as it's more popularly known, FireWire. With the camcorder turned off, connect its FireWire output to the computer input. This

Take some notes while you watch, describe the footage, its quality, and even possible ideas as to how it will all cut together. At first, do this with paper, but as you rack up more editing time, you'll be surprised how easy this is to do in your head. Jeffrey used to shoot and cut news and rarely kept a note. When he was shooting, he was editing the story in his head. Douglas has a custom notepad with timecode hints and a comment field that lets him make notes which are highly useful for long projects.

Both programs support capturing "live" from a DV source. Switch to camera mode, and the current picture displays ready for capture. Be aware that the audio picked up by the camera mic may feed back through your computer speakers, so turn them down first. Obviously, you must capture manually (video or stills) with this technique.

To help prevent dropping frames during capture, reduce the size of the capture window to a very small size. Also, turn off or temporarily disable background applications such as an Internet connection or antivirus software. Capture moves a lot of data between the camcorder and the computer. It's best not to let anything interfere with that formidable task. Defragmenting the capture hard drive before the session can also improve capture performance.

usually requires a four-pin to six-pin cable for desktops and four-pin to four-pin for connecting to a laptop. If you use a DV deck instead of a camcorder, use its FireWire output.

Turn on the camcorder or deck. Windows should recognize the device. Close the Windows dialog box at this point. Typically the camcorder should be in VCR mode, *not* camera (check your camcorder's documentation for details). Some cameras might require that the menu be set to digital output.

To capture analog video either connect the analog source, such a VHS to a camcorder or to an external capture device, such as the ADS Pyro A/V Link. Connect the camcorder or ADS to the computer via its FireWire connection, turn it on, and proceed.

Basic Capture

With the Media Pool open, and the proper bin selected, click the Capture video button or use File>Capture Video to launch the Video Capture utility. The Verify Tape Name dialog displays. Enter a name for the tape and then choose from the three available options.

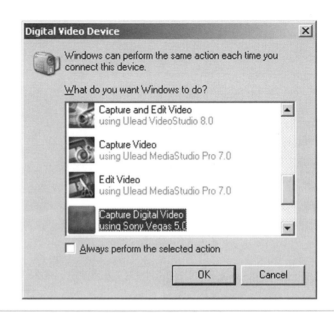

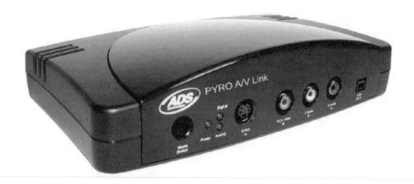

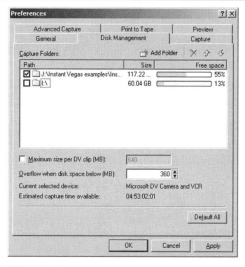

The capture utility has three main tabs: Capture, Advanced Capture, and Print to Tape. There is also a Preview window with transports controls. Along the bottom, the Clip Explorer functions like the Media Pool.

Note: Print to Tape is explained later in this book.

Movie Studio Users: There is no Advanced Capture capability available.

Before capturing clips, click Options> Preferences>Disk Management.

Determine where to store the captured files. We recommend you have a dedicated media hard drive separate from the C drive. Click the "Add Folder" button and use the dialog box to indicate this capture location. Create a new folder, if needed, by clicking the "Make New Folder" button. Click OK to close the dialog box.

You can create many capture folders and activate them by placing a check mark adjacent to the path. To deactivate a folder, remove the check mark. To delete a folder, click the "Remove Selected Folder" button or press Delete on the keyboard.

If the screen says "Please connect a device," double-check the connections. If that seems fine, try cycling the camcorder off and then back on again. If all is well, the screen should read "Device connected."

Notice the available free space indicator and the estimated capture time available. The format is hours:minutes:seconds;frames.

With the Preferences dialog box still open, switch to the Capture tab (Options>Preferences>Capture). Clear the check box "Enable DV scene detection" if you wish to turn this feature off (it is *on* by default). DV scene detection will attempt to capture scene changes to individual files.

With a DV device connected, notice that there is remote control over its transport functions: Play, Pause, Stop, Step backward left, step forward right, rewind, fast-forward. There is also a scrubber control.

Movie Studio Users: There is no scrubber tool available.

Above the transport controls are three choices: Capture Video, Capture Tape, and Capture Image.

Capture Video—This is the equivalent of a record button. Play the tape and click this button to record what you see on screen. Click stop to quit capturing.

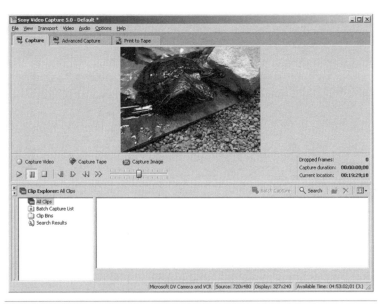

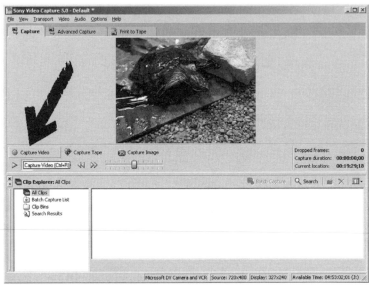

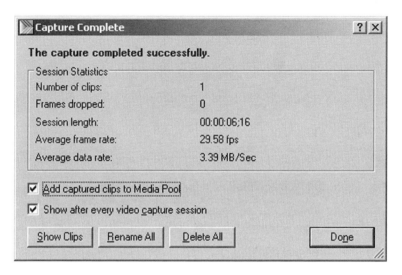

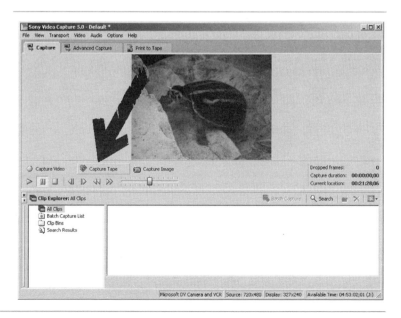

The Capture Complete dialog box displays important information about the capture session, including whether you dropped or lost any frames.

- Show Clips—displays thumbnails of what you captured.

- Rename All—changes the base name of the clips.

- Delete All—removes the clips.

- Done—accepts the clips and adds them to the Clip Bin. Check the box to add the captured clips to the Media Pool, too.

Capture Tape—Click this to capture the entire tape in one session. The software rewinds the tape, if necessary, and records everything on the tape. Consider enabling DV scene detection in Preferences (as explained above) to automatically chop the tape into shorter chunks. The Capture Complete dialog displays at the end of this session, too.

Capture Image—Navigate to the still you want to capture on the tape and click Capture Image. Vegas and Vegas Movie Studio capture a still in JPEG (JPG) or Bitmap (BMP) file format.

If you get dropped frames, you may need to recapture. Unfortunately, the software doesn't tell you where those lost frames are. You'll have to manually hunt them down. If you get a garbled capture when starting at the beginning of a tape, let the tape play for a couple seconds until the digital information is stable.

Be aware that blanks spaces on the tape can confuse the Capture Tape setting into thinking the tape is over. If you have these gaps, caused by not stopping and restarting the tape in the same place, you may need to capture manually. Keep timecode on the tape for best results.

If you prefer to save stills as bitmaps (BMP), use Options>Preferences>Capture and clear the "Save captured stills as JPEG" check box.

To automatically deinterlace captured stills, check the "Deinterlace image when capturing stills" check box in Options>Preferences>Capture. This is a good practice.

Use Capture Still for stop-motion animation and time-lapse sequences. Both Vegas and Vegas Movie Studio capture and sequentially number individual frames. Later you can import this image sequence as one event on the Timeline.

Avoid capturing clips exactly where you plan to edit them. Instead leave some handles, or extra time, at the beginning and ending of each clip. In short, your clip I/O can be rather loose.

Advanced Capture

There are many advantages to using Advanced Capture. One, you can log tapes and only capture those shots you deem worthy. Two, you can batch-capture after creating the capture list. Three, you can easily recapture media in the future if you save the Video Capture file.

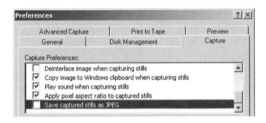

Click the Advanced Capture tab to access the controls. If the Verify Tape Name dialog displays, enter a name for the tape. It's a good practice to use the same exact name as what is on the actual DV tape.

The screen looks essentially the same except for the new section to the right. With Advanced Capture, you manually scrub the tape, locate the clips you

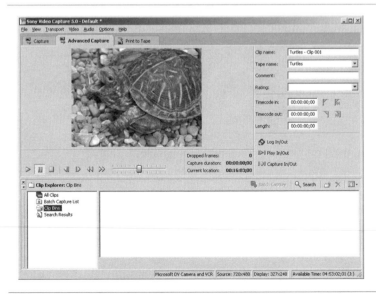

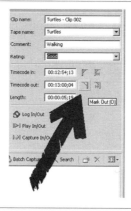

want, name them, enter the clip's start (in) and finish (out) point, and then log these data. This builds the Batch Capture list for automatic, unattended capture. Alternately, you can immediately capture the clip manually.

It's acceptable to enter a clip's out-point before its in-point.

Use the transport controls to locate the start of the clip you wish to capture.

- Clip name: Enter a name for the clip. The software suggests a name based on the tape name and the clip number (which sequentially number automatically). Accept these defaults or enter a more meaningful name.

- Tape name: Choose the tape currently in the camcorder.

- Comment: Enter an optional note about the clip.

- Rating: Choose a rating from the drop-down list.

Click the Mark In button or use the I keyboard shortcut.

Navigate to the end of the clip and click the Mark Out button or use the O keyboard shortcut. Notice the length of the clip displays.

After programming the in- and out-points, there are three choices:

- Log In/Out—adds the clip to the Batch Capture List.

- Play In/Out—plays the clip.

- Capture In/Out—captures the clip immediately.

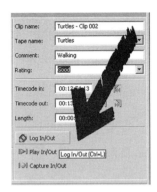

When using Advanced Capture, save and name the session. Should you need to re-capture clips, simply recall the file, put in the appropriate tape, and start the Batch Capture again.

Continue to log your tapes, repeating the above workflow until finished.

If you choose to batch-capture your tape, click the Batch Capture button in the Clip Explorer's right pane to initiate the capture process after you've programmed the list. Vegas will start the capture process. This works automatically and doesn't require your attention. The Capture Complete dialog box displays when the batch process finishes so you can check for any errors.

Scanning Photographs and Other Graphics

Many videos use still images and graphics to tell their story. To get this pre-existing media into your computer, you'll need a flatbed scanner and its associated software installed.

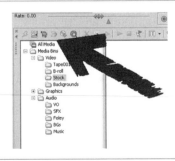

With the Media Pool open, and a bin created and selected, click the Get photo button or File>Get photo to launch your scanning software.

Refer to your scanner's instructions for specific details.

Though you can use any supported file format, we suggest saving files in PNG format for best results.

Computers use square pixels, while DV uses rectangles (.909 of square). If you prepare media in a photo editing or other graphics program, resize them to 720×576 or 655×480 (PAL: 704×576) to compensate for the NLE's square-to-rectangle conversion. Double that size if you plan to zoom in on the graphic.

Saving in PNG format is again the best choice because the format supports alpha channel information which both Vegas and Vegas Movie Studio recognize. Alpha channels are clear or transparent backgrounds which make compositing them over video a snap. PNG is an ideal format for logos, lower-thirds, and other effects.

Video's resolution is 72dpi so it doesn't make sense to scan photographs or graphics at any resolution higher than 150dpi.

Media with an alpha channel has a gray checkboard background in both the Media Pool and the Timeline. Vegas will usually recognize alpha information in a graphic file.

Extract Audio from CD

If you have purchased sound effects or production library music that comes on audio CDs, insert the disc, create or select a Media Pool bin, and click the Extract Audio from CD button or choose File>Extract Audio from CD.

Vegas and Vegas Movie Studio users can join Vegas Movie Studio (www.screenblast. com) and get access to music, sound effects, and stock footage for a nominal yearly fee.

From the dialog box, select choices from the Action drop-down list. Options include extracting individual tracks, a time range, or the entire CD. The play button previews selections.

Movie Studio Users: There is support only for extracting tracks.

After making selections, click OK. The Save As dialog box displays. Name the file or accept the suggested name, choose a location on the hard drive to store the file, and click OK.

Get Media from the Web

The last button in the Media Pool, Get Media from the Web, launches your web browser and takes you to a special section of the Sony site (or the Vegas Movie Studio site). Here you can download free media along with links to media for sale.

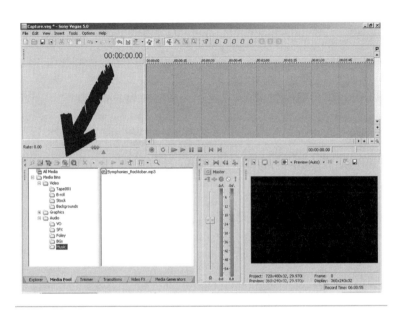

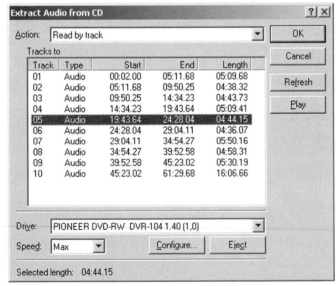

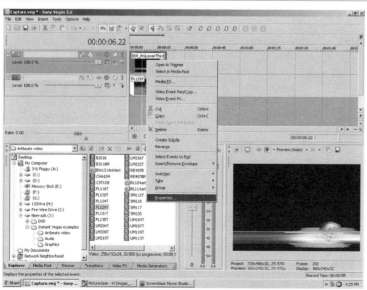

Adding Third-Party Material

Stock footage, such as the Artbeats collections used in this book, along with animations and other video eye candy, work well in both Vegas and Vegas Movie Studio. Typically, this material arrives on CD-ROMs or DVD-ROMs ready to use. We suggest copying the files to the hard drive before adding them to your projects.

Some products require processing the disc files with software into a format compatible with the NLEs. Choose the AVI format and the Full Frame (Uncompressed) codec to save the processed file to your hard drive. This format maintains alpha, or transparent, channel information for easy compositing in Vegas and Vegas Movie Studio.

If a processed Digital Juice graphic doesn't appear with its alpha channel (the background is black instead of the gray checkerboard pattern), right-click the event on the Timeline or in the Media Pool, and choose Properties.

Click the Media tab and set the Alpha channel to "Straight (unmatted)" by choosing from the drop-down list, then click OK.

The Future of Capture

The capture process as described above will soon be replaced. Today there are small FireWire HDs that connect directly to camcorders and record in real time. When the shoot finishes, simply connect the drive to the computer and edit. Though you still need to log and review your footage, the capture process is eliminated.

Firestore and Serious Magic also manufacture tapeless capture tools. Firestore is a hard-drive-based system, while Serious Magic's DV Rack is a software system.

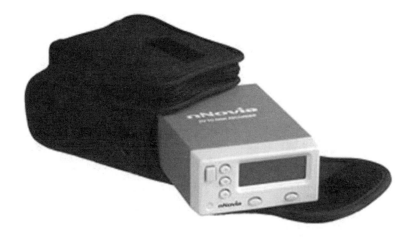

Chapter 4

Slicing, Dicing, and Cooking Creative

Time to start building your project by adding media to the Timeline, creating audio and video tracks, and discovering the basic editing techniques.

Though video and audio reside on separate tracks, the software treats them equally as events. And as events, the principles discussed in this chapter apply whether it is a video or audio event. Where they differ, it will be so noted.

Adding Tracks and Media to the Timeline

To create a video track on the Vegas Timeline, click Insert>Video Track or use the Ctrl+Shift+Q keyboard short-cut. To create an audio track, click Insert>Audio Track or use the Ctrl+Q keyboard shortcut. You can also right-click inside the track header area to insert either audio or video tracks.

Movie Studio Users: There are the maximum three audio and video tracks already in place.

Add media to the Timeline using either the Media Pool, Explorer, or Trimmer. The Media Pool and Explorer work similarly. Left-click to select the file, hold down the mouse button, drag the file to the applicable track on the Timeline, and release the mouse button. Also, use Shift+click or Ctrl+click to select and add multiple media files.

Double-clicking a file in Explorer or Media Pool using the left mouse button will also add it to the selected track at the current cursor position. If a video file has audio associated with it, the audio will be added to an adjacent audio track automatically.

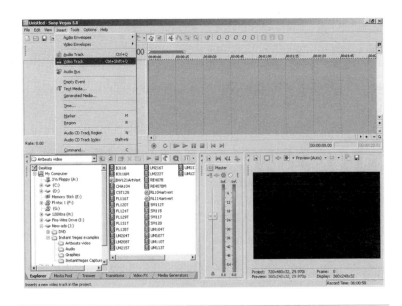

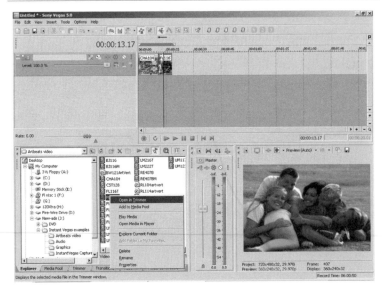

To move a file to the Trimmer, right-click the media file in Explorer and choose either "Open in Trimmer" (or "Add to Media Pool.")

Right-click a file in the Media Pool and choose "Open in Trimmer."

Movie Studio Users: The Trimmer isn't available in this version.

Vegas editors use the Trimmer for two main reasons:

- To fine-tune, or trim, the edges of a media event.

- To add multiple shorter sections from a longer event to the project. For example, splitting the best parts from a single long interview into a more concise segment.

You do *not* have to use the Trimmer (Douglas rarely does), because Vegas (and Vegas Movie Studio) allow trimming and splitting events on the Timeline. See below.

Before adding a file using the Trimmer, make a time selection. There are two methods.

Play the clip and enter I for the in- or start point and then hit O for the out- or stop point. Notice the bar along the

Vegas does not require creating tracks before adding media. Drag a media file to an empty space on the Timeline. The software creates the appropriate track automatically, placing the media on it.

Drag a file from either Explorer or the Media Pool to the Trimmer tab to open the file in the Trimmer, too.

top of the Trimmer window. Double-click this time selection to select it. Blue lines appear at the ends.

The Trimmer remembers your last five time selections. Use the keyboard Backspace key to cycle through them.

The other method is to position the cursor above the Trimmer ruler and click and drag a time selection.

Once you've made a time selection, click the media inside the selection and drag it to the Timeline. Alternately, click the "Add Media from Cursor" button or use the A keyboard shortcut. This puts the media time selection on the selected track at the cursor position forward.

Click the Add media up to cursor, keyboard shortcut Ctrl+A, to put media on the selected Timeline track up to (before) the cursor position.

Right-Click Add Media Options

There is additional power when dragging files from Explorer, Media Pool, or Trimmer using a right-mouse-button click and drag. Select a media file using either Explorer, Media Pool, or Trimmer. Press and hold the right mouse button and drag to the Timeline. A dialog box pops up.

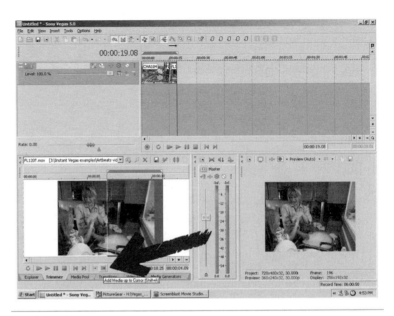

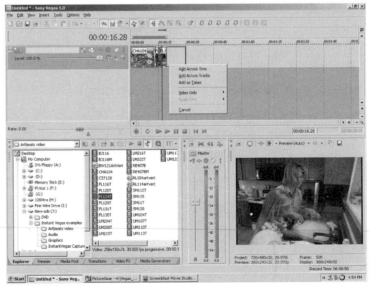

The results of these options vary depending on whether you add a single file or multiple files.

Vegas right-click add single media file options and results:

- Add Across Time—places the event along the Timeline forward.

- Add Across Tracks—creates a new track and places the event in it.

- Add as Takes—in this case, places the event along the Timeline forward (see below).

- Video Only—performs one of the above operations for only the video portion of a file.

- Audio Only—performs one of the above operations for only the audio portion of a file.

- Cancel

Vegas right-click add multiple media files options and results:

- Add Across Time—places the events one after another on the Timeline.

- Add Across Tracks—creates new tracks and places each event in its own track at the same position.

- Add as Takes—places each event on top of one another in one track as a virtual stack. Only one event can be seen or heard at a time. Press T to cycle through the takes and events.

- Video Only—performs one of the above operations for only the video portion of the files.

- Audio Only—performs one of the above operations for only the audio portion of the files.

- Cancel

Vegas Movie Studio right-click add media files options and results:

- Add—places the event(s) on the Timeline.

- Add as Takes—stacks events on top of each other (T cycles through them).

- Ripple Insert—explained later in this book.

- Video Only—affects video only with Add and Add as Takes options.

- Audio Only—affects audio only with Add and Add as Takes options.

- Cancel

Here's yet another method. Right-click media in the Vegas Trimmer and select from the options:

- Select Video and Audio

- Select Video Only (Tab)

- Select Audio Only (Shift+Tab)

Then, use the "Add Media from Cursor" or "Add Media up to Cursor" button.

Select a track and then make a time selection on the Timeline. Switch to the Trimmer and click the "Add Media from Cursor" button to fill the Timeline time selection with the media from the Trimmer.

Moving events

Move an event on the Timeline by selecting it and dragging it into position.

Butt one event right next to another for a straight cut. Use care to not leave tiny gaps between events. Zoom in closer to be sure your edits are accurate. You can also use Ripple to remove blank spaces, or you can use scripts to help locate blank areas. We'll talk more about rippling later.

To avoid this issue, enable snapping by either clicking the Toolbar icon or using Options>Enable Snapping (F8). Make sure Quantize to Frames, Snap to Grid, and Snap to Markers are enabled, too.

Movie Studio Users: Quantize to Frames is called Snap to Frames.

Move events with the number keypad with Num Lock enabled.

- 2—moves the event down vertically to the next adjacent track.

- 4—moves the event left horizontally.

- 6—moves the event right horizontally .

- 8—moves the event up vertically to the next adjacent track.

You can cut, copy, and paste Timeline events, too.

Need to duplicate *and* move an event? Select it and hold down the Ctrl key while you drag the copied event to a new position. The original remains in place. Vegas will ask if you want to reference the original event or create a new one. If you want to be able to modify the new or original event, select Create New Copy.

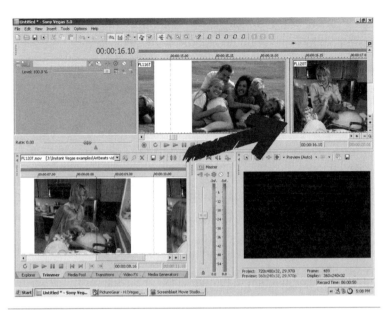

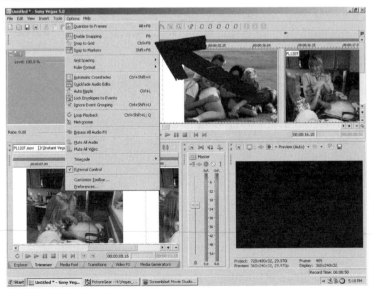

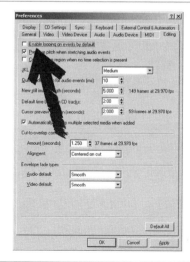

Timeline Trimming and Splitting

To change the start and end points of a piece of media, select the event on the Timeline by clicking it.

Vegas shows the edge frame in the Preview window as you trim the event.

Position the cursor at either edge. Notice how the cursor changes. Click and drag in to shorten events; click and drag out to lengthen events.

If you drag an event past its end, the event starts over or loops. The tiny divot at the top of the event indicates the loop point.

Click Options>Preferences>Editing and uncheck the "Enable looping on events by default." Now when you drag an event past its end point, the last frame holds for as long as you extend the event (note that the loop divot still appears).

We prefer to leave looping enabled. To override this global setting, right-click the event and choose Properties. In the dialog box, uncheck the loop check box and click OK. This event will no longer loop (and instead hold its last frame when extended). You can also override this with the Switches dialog found when you right-click the event.

To break a larger event into two pieces, position the cursor where you want to split the event. Click Edit>Split or the handy keyboard shortcut S.

Remember that NLE editing is non-destructive. Trimming, splitting, and other effects do not affect the original files in any way. They remain intact on the computer.

Movie Studio Users: Click the Split Event button on the toolbar.

There are now two separate events.

Split events into as many pieces as needed. These separate events can be moved, copied, deleted and more—just as any other event.

Event Envelopes

Each event has its own envelope that control several features. Video event envelopes include fade in, fade out, opacity, and velocity. Audio event envelopes include fade in, fade out, and event volume level.

Video

Select a video event on the Timeline. Position the cursor near the top left edge. Notice that the cursor changes to a pie shape with arrows.

Hold the mouse button and drag to the right. This adds a fade-in. Note the curved white line.

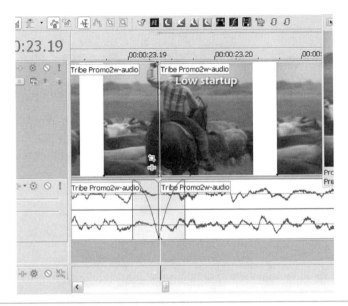

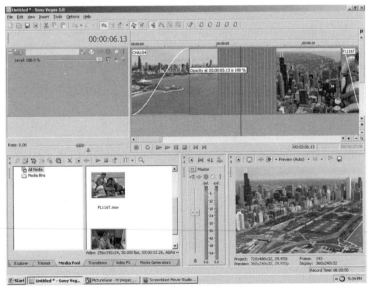

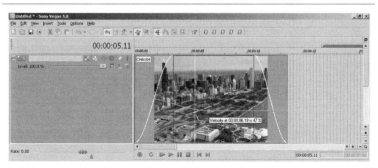

Position the cursor near the top right edge of the same event. Note the cursor change.

Hold the mouse button and drag to the left to add a fade-out.

Speeding up or slowing down an event affects its length. Trim and adjust manually.

Right-click either fade and choose Fade Type from the pop-up menu. Select from the choices to affect how the fade envelope progresses over time.

Next, position the cursor near the top of the video event (away from the fades). The cursor changes to a pointing hand.

Click and drag down to change the opacity of the event. This allows a top event to superimpose over another event on a lower track; the lower track shows, too.

Right-click the video event and choose Insert/Remove Envelope>Velocity from the pop-up menu.

Movie Studio Users: Velocity is not available on events.

Vegas places a green line through the event. This envelope controls velocity or the speed of the event.

Move the line up for fast motion; down for slow motion. Move it past the zero point (to negative percentages) to reverse the event. Reverse also can be slow or fast.

Double-click the velocity envelope to add a point or right-click and choose Add Point. Click and drag this point to a new setting.

Manipulating the points over time gives you immense creative control. Add as many points and drag them to new settings as necessary to achieve the effect you're after.

Right-click a point (or the line between points) for more options, including ones to control how Vegas transitions between points.

Audio

Select an audio event on the Timeline. Position the cursor near the top left edge. Notice that the cursor changes to a quarter pie shape with arrows.

Hold the mouse button and drag to the right to fade in the sound. Note the white line.

Popular today is a single shot that starts in fast motion and abruptly changes to slow motion. The velocity envelope is the tool to achieve this look.

To quickly reverse an event (audio or video) in Vegas 5, right-click it and choose Reverse from the pop-up menu.

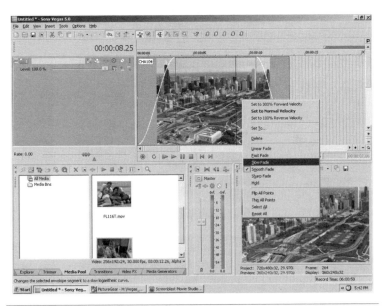

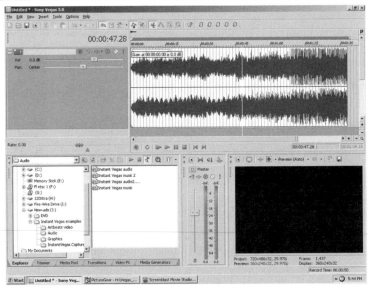

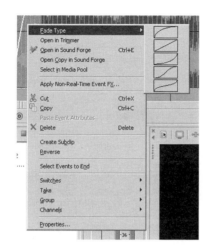

Position the cursor near the top right edge of the same event. Note the cursor change.

Hold the mouse button and drag to the left to add a fade-out.

Right-click either fade and choose Fade Type from the pop-up menu. Select from the choices to affect how the fade envelope sounds over time.

Next, position the cursor at the top of the audio event (away from the fades). The cursor changes to a pointing hand.

Musicians may feel that the fade-in, volume level, and fade-out look familiar. It's the NLE equivalent of attack, sustain, and release (ASR).

The amount of event overlap determines the transition's time length.

Click and drag down to change the volume level of the event. Notice how the amplitude (height) of the waveform changes as you pull down the line.

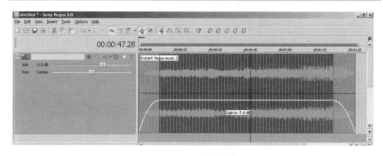

Transitions

Turn on Automatic Crossfades (it's on by default) by clicking the Toolbar icon or using the Ctrl+Shift+X shortcut.

Move one event so it overlaps another on the Timeline. Notice that the X that appears, signifying a crossfade.

Play the Timeline to see how one event fades out while the other fades in. If this is an audio event, listen for the change.

Video events can have a variety of transitions applied to the crossfades. Click the Transitions tab in the Windows docking area. There are dozens of transitions from which to choose.

Click a transition and drag and drop it on the crossfade created above.

The dialog box that displays provides control over the transition's properties. Make any necessary changes then close the dialog box.

Click Play to preview the result.

Experiment by trying out other transitions to see how they look with your video.

Transitions are *not* relegated for use only between events. Add a fade-in or fade-out to a single video event. Drag a transition and drop it on the fade to apply it to the single event.

Right-click the transition and choose Transition Properties from the pop-up menu to make other changes, if needed.

Right-click the Transition and choose Fade Type and then select from the graphics which envelopes you want to use. Experiment to understand the differences.

Vegas users can hold down the Shift key when dragging and dropping a transition to bypass the transition dialog box.

Click above the ruler and drag to create a time selection around the section you're working on. When you play the Timeline, only that section will play, then stop. (When gray in color. If blue, the selected area will loop.)

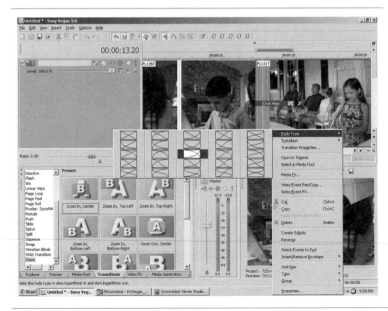

Vegas 5 Transition Envelopes

Right-click a transition and choose Insert/Remove Envelope>Transition Progress.

This inserts an envelope over the transition.

Add points (right-click and choose Add Point) and position them to affect how the transition changes over time. Some unique effects are available through this tool, such as a split screen wipe that never finishes.

Slip Trim Events

Often there is a video clip event that is the right length on the Timeline, but you want to adjust where it starts and ends *within* the clip.

Select an event and hover the mouse pointer over it. Don't hover over the cursor, though. Press and hold the Alt key. The mouse pointer changes to a box with two arrows in it. Left-click the mouse button and drag (while still pressing Alt).

The video preview is a split screen. This shows the event starting frame on the left and its ending frame on the right. The event stays in place, but the video within changes.

To slip trim one edge, click the opposite event edge, press and hold Alt, and drag.

Slip trims work best on clips that have already been edge-trimmed. Slip trimming a whole event may introduce a loop point.

Again, the split screen shows both the start and end. One edge remains fixed, while the other slip-trims.

To both move and slip trim an event, hold down Ctrl+Alt while dragging the event.

Movie Studio Users: There is no split screen preview when slip trimming.

Ripple Editing

Sometimes you need one edit change to affect everything else after it. In other words, you want the edit to ripple down the Timeline. For example, you want to paste a new event between two existing ones with the whole project sliding down to make room. Ripple edit mode to the rescue.

Turn on Auto Ripple by clicking the Toolbar icon or using the keyboard shortcut Ctrl+L.

Movie Studio Users: Ripple edits work when using cut, copy, and paste on the Timeline. Ripple insert is also an option when you right-click add media file. The ripples affect events on only one selected track.

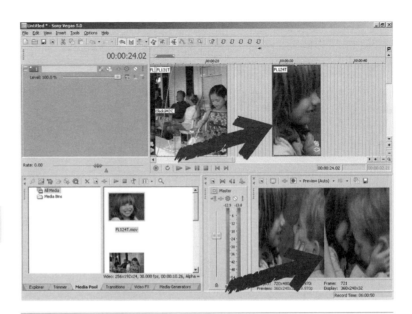

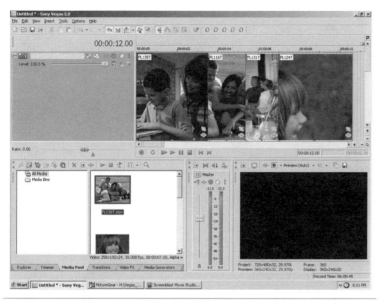

Vegas gives you three ripple edit modes from which to choose.

- Affected Tracks

- Affected Tracks, Bus Tracks, Markers, and Regions

- All Tracks, Markers, and Regions

With an existing project displayed, drag a new event and place it in between two others, and release.

Notice how the other events move down.

If you leave the Auto Ripple off, Vegas lets you perform a post edit ripple, too. After making the edit, use one of these keyboard shortcuts:

- F—Affected Tracks

- Ctrl+F—Affected Tracks, Bus Tracks, Markers, and Regions

- Ctrl+Shift+F—All Tracks, Markers, and Regions

Shuffle Events

Quickly reorder events on the Timeline.

Right-click an event, drag it to a new location, and release. Choose Shuffle Events from the pop-up menu.

Ripple edits work when you move, cut, copy, paste, trim, and add media to the Timeline.

Auto Ripple mode coupled to keypad trimming make Timeline trimming fast and easy.

Double-click in between events, turn on Ripple, and press Delete or Ctrl+X to delete the hole and perfectly butt two events together. Douglas creates selections that he'd like to delete, presses the S key to split out a section, and then Ctrl+X to delete and ripple all at the same time.

Time Selections

Click and drag above the ruler to make a time selection.

Both Vegas and Vegas Movie Studio remember the last five time selections. Use the keyboard Backspace key to cycle through them.

Click the Loop icon in the Transport section or use the Q shortcut to toggle looping on and off.

The time selection changes colors to dark blue. Position the cursor inside the selection and click Play. The section will repeat endlessly until stopped.

Double-click an event to create a time selection exactly to size.

Double-click a transition to create a time selection the length of the transition. This is useful for checking the transition's duration ensuring uniformity for certain projects.

Below the Timeline, to the far right of the transport controls, are three boxes. The first indicates the start of the time selection; the second the end. The third shows the duration of the selection.

Double-click any of the boxes and type a value as needed.

If there is no time selection, the first box indicates the cursor position. Double-click and type a value to quickly move the cursor. Ctrl+G quickly highlights the box for data entry, too.

Markers and Regions

Time selections are temporary and always evolving. Use markers and regions as more permanent indicators. Markers and regions are the NLE equivalent of sticky notes. They appear just above the time selection area at the top of the Timeline.

Make a time selection and click Insert> Region or press R. Type a name for the Region and then press Enter.

To mark a single point in time, position the cursor and press M to insert a marker. Give it a name and press enter.

To move a marker, or either edge of a region, click and drag it to the new position.

Right-click a marker or region for additional options.

Need to check an edit fast? Position the cursor and press zero (0) on the keypad. Vegas creates a time selection centered around the cursor and then plays the selection automatically. Set the time selection amount in Options>Preferences>Editing>Cursor preview duration.

Markers can be inserted while a project plays in real time, too. Just press M while the time indicator is moving.

Jump right to one of the first 10 markers or regions by using the corresponding 1–0 keys on the keyboard (not keypad). You may also move between markers by clicking in the Marker bar and using the left and right arrows to navigate from marker to marker.

Chapter 5

More Editing Wizardry

Beyond the basic editing procedures are a variety of tools that bring many creative possibilities to your projects. These include effects, compositing, picture-in-picture looks, movement on stills, and more.

Effects (FX)

FX fall into two categories: utility and creative. Generally, utility effects fix something wrong with your video or audio. Creative effects typically take your project to a new level, lending artistic qualities to your video. However, some effects can be used both ways.

Video Effects

Place video effects on tracks, individual video events, or the project as a whole.

Movie Studio Users: Video FX apply only to individual events and the project as a whole.

To add video FX at the track level, click the Track FX button on a video track header. All events on the track will have the same FX applied.

The Video Track FX Plug-in Chooser is displayed.

Select the FX and click Add.

You can add multiple effects into what's called a plug-in chain, too.

Alternately, click the Video FX tab in the window docking area. The left pane lists the video FX available; the right shows various animated presets. Scroll through the options to choose.

Either click a Video FX name from the left pane or a preset from the right pane and drag and drop it on a video track header.

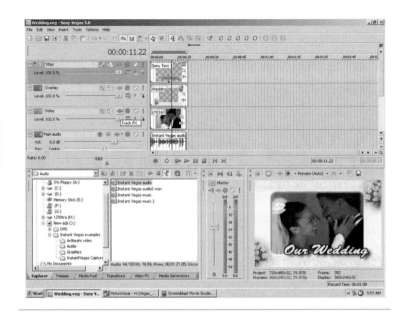

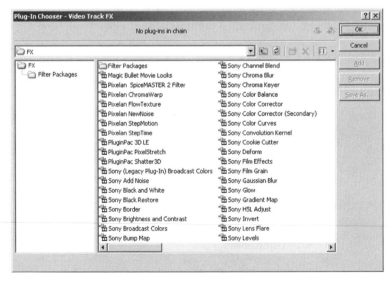

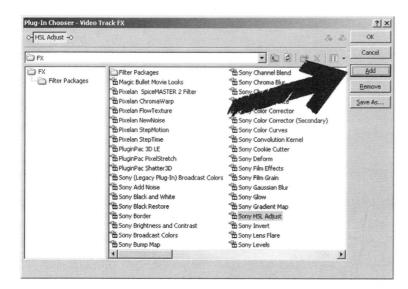

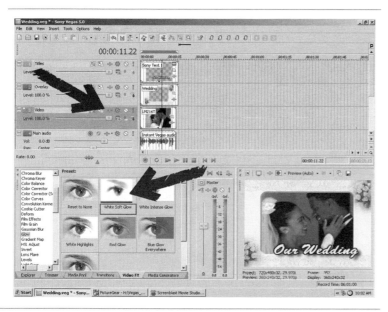

The dialog box for the FX parameters is displayed. Make adjustments as needed and close the dialog box.

To add FX to a single event, click its Event FX button. Only the selected event will have this FX applied.

If an event's duration is very short or if the project is lengthy and zoomed in, the Event FX button may not be displayed. Either zoom in to reveal the Event FX button or right-click and choose Video Event FX from the pop-up menu.

The Video Event FX Plug-in Chooser is displayed. Make your choices as described above.

You can also drag and drop FX from the Video FX tab of the window docking area directly on to a video event.

Movie Studio Users: There is no Edit Chain button on the Event Video FX dialog. However, you can drag and drop additional effects from the window docking area video FX tab to this dialog to build a chain.

To add FX to the entire project, click the Video Output FX button in the Preview window.

Hold down Shift while dragging and dropping FX to bypass its parameters dialog box.

The Video Output FX Plug-in Chooser displays. Make your choices as described above.

Drag and drop any FX from the Video FX tab of the window docking area directly on to the Preview window, too.

Audio Effects

Place audio effects on tracks, buses, as assignable FX, or the whole project.

Movie Studio Users: Apply audio FX only to tracks and the master Audio. Vegas Movie Studio does not offer Bus assignments.

To add audio FX at the track level, click the Track FX button on an audio track header. All audio events on the track will have the same FX applied.

The Audio Plug-in dialog displays. Notice there are three audio effects already in the plug-in chain.

- Track Noise Gate—shuts out noise below a certain threshold setting.

- Track EQ—shapes the tonal characteristics of sound.

- Track Compressor—changes the dynamics of sound.

Video Output FX are generally good for global settings such as making an entire video black and white, adding timecode window burn to a project, or setting legal colors with the NTSC Broadcast filter.

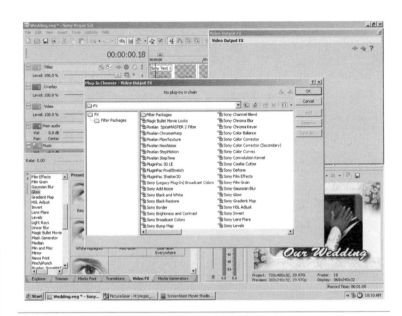

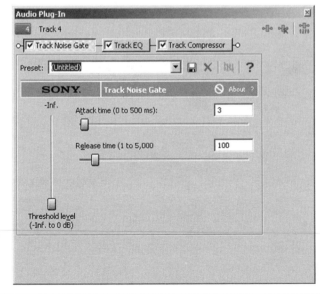

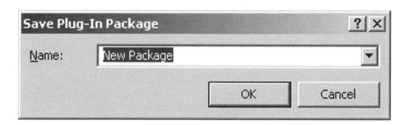

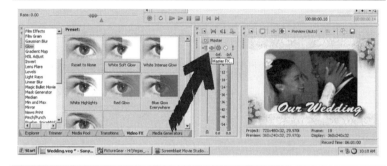

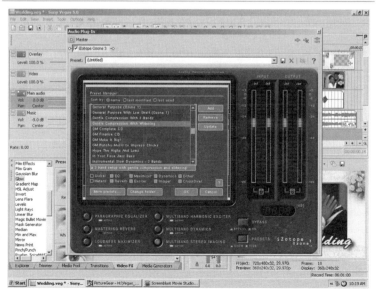

Movie Studio Users: Only the ExpressFX Equalization plug-in displays initially.

Click the Plug-In Chain button to add additional effects.

Movie Studio Users: Click Edit Chain to add additional audio FX.

The Plug-in Chooser dialog displays. Navigate to plug-ins to apply and click Add to append them to the chain.

To save a plug-in chain, preserving all settings, click Save As and name the package in the resulting dialog. Recall FX packages from the Plug-in Chooser dialog as described above.

To add audio effects to the master (or other buses), click the Master FX (or Bus FX) button.

The Plug-in Chooser dialog displays. Make selections, add them to the chain, and choose OK.

The dialog box for the chosen plug-ins displays. Tweak the parameters as needed.

To bypass FX, remove the check mark adjacent the plug-in name on its button.

To rearrange a plug-in chain (in the Plug-in Chooser), click, drag, and release the plug-in's button to a new location in the chain. After setting plug-in priority and which plug-ins are to be used, right-click the track header and select "Set Default Track Properties" so that Vegas can remember which plug-ins you want on each new audio track. Douglas has removed Noise Gate from his default chain and substituted the WAVES compressor for the Sony compressor.

Using Vegas audio buses and assignable effects are discussed later in this book.

Right-click any FX button for a short-cut menu.

Right-click any slider in an FX dialog and choose Presets from the pop-up menu.

- Bypass All—turns off the FX, leaving them in place.

- Enable All—turns on bypassed FX.

- Delete All—deletes all FX in the chain.

- Plug-in Chooser—displays the Plug-in Chooser dialog.

Vegas shows bypassed FX in the track header, on busses, and the Preview window.

Using FX Presets

Consider the video and audio FX presets as starting points.

Access video presets from the Window docking Video FX tab. Drag and drop them as needed.

Additionally, after adding video FX to a track, event, or project, click the corresponding FX button. Choose from the Presets drop-down list.

Audio effects plug-ins also have Presets. Click a Track FX button to display the dialog and choose presets from the drop-down list.

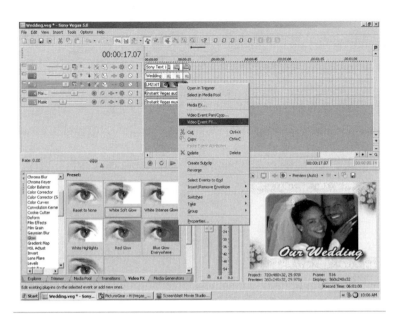

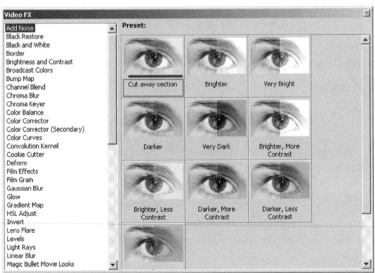

You can save and later recall your own FX presets (audio and video). After making changes with the dialog, click the Preset box and type in a unique name.

Next, click the Save Preset button.

To delete a Preset, call it up from the drop-down list and click the Delete Preset button.

Using Keyframes to Change Video FX over Time

You can change video FX, and many other Vegas and Vegas Movie Studio functions, over time using keyframes. The term keyframe essentially means a point in time with specific settings. Your wristwatch is a good example of a keyframe. You have specific behaviors at a point in time. To change an effect over time requires two keyframes. However, you can add as many keyframes as needed to achieve the effect you want.

Movie Studio Users: There are only two keyframes available: begin and end.

Add an effect, such as 25 percent Black and White preset, to a video event. The Video Event FX dialog displays.

The keyframe Timeline for the effect appears along the bottom of the dialog box. The available options include:

Each FX in a video chain will have its own keyframe Timeline lane.

- Sync Cursor—toggles showing the cursor in the keyframe Timeline at the time same position as the regular Timeline cursor.

- First Keyframe—navigates to the first keyframe.

- Previous/Next Keyframe—moves to the nearest keyframe in the direction specified.

- Last Keyframe—navigates to the last keyframe.

- Create keyframe—places a keyframe at the cursor position (shortcut Insert key).

- Delete keyframe—deletes the selected keyframe (shortcut Delete key).

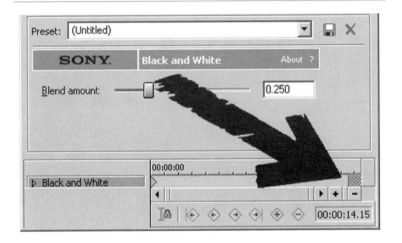

Place the cursor near the end of the keyframe Timeline.

Click the Insert Keyframe button and notice the diamond that appears. You do not need to click the Insert Keyframe button, as simply changing an FX setting will automatically insert the keyframe at the cursor position.

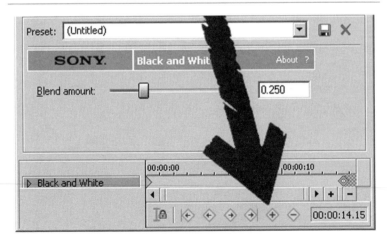

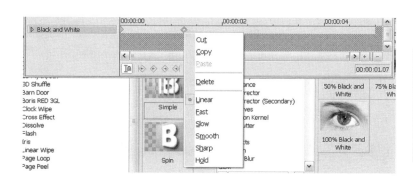

Drag the "Blend amount" slider to 1.000.

Play the event to see it start in color and slowly fade to black and white.

Movie Studio Users: Click the Begin button and set the effect to taste. Click the End button and set the new effect parameters. Vegas Movie Studio will transition between the start and end settings automatically.

To control how Vegas transitions between keyframes, right-click a keyframe and choose from the options: Linear, Fast, Slow, Smooth, Sharp, and Hold. The first five gradually change to the new keyframe setting in different ways. Hold instantly changes to a new setting.

Vegas keyframes can be moved, cut, copied, and pasted as needed. Draw a rectangle in the keyframe lane to select all keyframes. Holding Alt while dragging the last selected keyframe will move all keyframes with linear distance between each keyframe.

Audio FX use envelopes to change over time (see below). The only exception is the surround sound panner, which uses keyframes.

Using envelopes to change audio FX over time

Click an audio track to select it and type V to insert a volume envelope. Notice the blue line that runs the entire length of the track. The envelope color may be changed in Options>Preferences>Display.

Double-click anywhere on the blue line

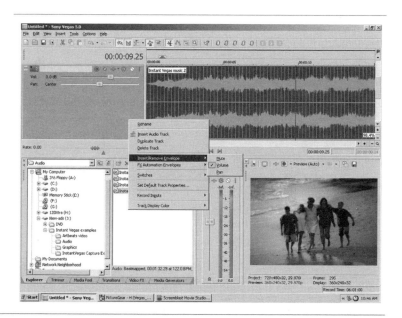

Envelopes can only boost 6dB maximum but cut to silence (-inf).

Certain audio effects are automatable, meaning they can change over time. Use envelopes to control these settings. These are discussed later in the book.

Video FX use keyframes to change over time (see above). The only exceptions are Mute, Opacity, Fade to Color, and Event Velocity and Transition Progress. These work the same as audio envelopes.

to add a point or right-click the line and choose Add Point. You can add as many points as needed; there is no limit.

Click and drag the point to a new position to change the envelope.

Right-click a point for additional options including quick preset settings.

Movie Studio Users: Only Volume and Pan envelopes are available.

Track volume envelopes are relative to the track fader. Zero (0) on the envelope corresponds to the fader setting. Positive envelope values add to the fader; negative envelope values subtract. For example, –12 on the fader with an envelope of –3 equals –15 at that point. Move the envelope to 6 and that equals –6 (-12+6) overall.

Right-click the line between points to choose the transition between points. Settings include several fade styles including Linear, Fast, Slow, Smooth, and Sharp. The Hold setting makes an immediate change.

Movie Studio Users: Only Linear, Fast, and Slow settings are available between points.

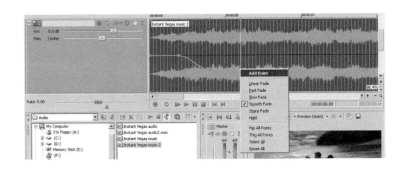

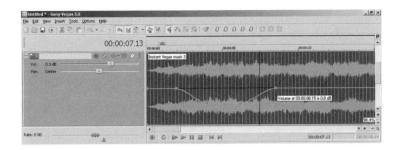

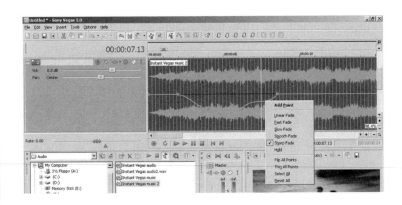

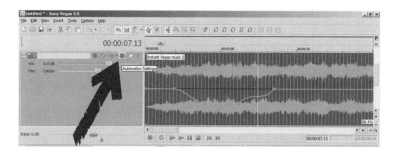

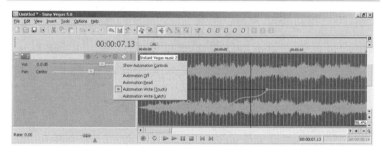

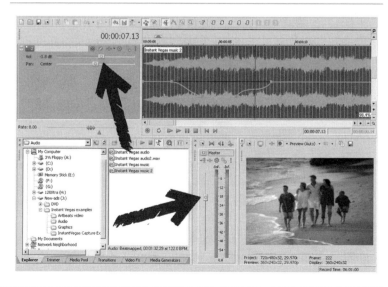

Vegas Automation

Real-time automation is new to Vegas 5. Parameters that can be controlled through envelopes can be controlled through real-time automation, too.

Video Automation

- Opacity

- Fade to color

- Mute

Audio Automation

- Volume

- Pan

- Mute

- FX automation

- Assignable FX sends

Click the Automation Settings in the track header. Choices include:

- Show Automation Controls—turns on automation for controllable parameters.

- Automation off—disables automation playback and recording.

- Automation Read—plays automation but does not allow recording new.

Vegas audio buses also have automation.

- Automation Write (Touch)—records and plays automation. When you release a control, the envelope returns to 0. This is often used for tweaking a mix.

- Automation Write (Latch)—records and plays automation. When you release a control, the envelope remains at the last setting. This is often used to set up a final mix.

Note that automatable controls now show the automation icon on them.

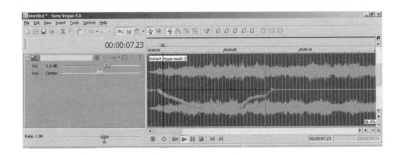

Play the Timeline and move an automatable control, volume for example, and adjust as the project plays.

Vegas draws an envelope that reflects the moves you made. You can add additional automation as needed.

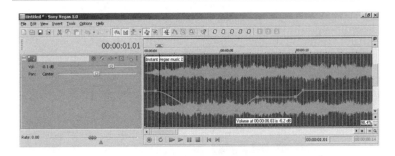

Also, you can edit these envelopes as described earlier.

If you have a device such as the Mackie Universal Control or other MIDI controller you can automate not only audio moves but also composite envelopes, effectively giving you an automated video switcher!

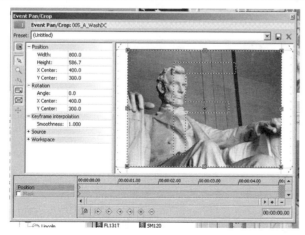

Crop, Rotate, and Reverse the Video Image

Both Vegas and Vegas Movie Studio provide sophisticated control over the look of every video event. You can crop, rotate, and reverse/flip the angle of any video event (including stills and other graphics).

Select an event and click its Event Pan/Crop button or right-click it and choose Video Event Pan/Crop from the pop-up menu.

The Event Pan/Crop dialog box displays. The event shows to the right with various controls on the left.

- Show properties—toggles showing and hiding the settings.

- Normal Edit Tool—controls the selection box.

- Zoom Edit Tool—zooms in and out on the event for fine-tuning selections.

- Enable snapping—snaps the selection box to the grid.

- Lock aspect ratio—resizing maintains the proper project aspect ratio.

- Size about center—toggles resizing around the center point or an edge.

- Move freely—toggles whether movement is constrained or not.

Movie Studio Users: Click the FX button and choose the Pan/Crop tab.

Event pan/crop is fully keyframable, meaning settings can be adjusted as the event plays.

Notice the selection box with handles and its letter F superimposed over the video event.

To crop the image, click and drag a handle to the size desired.

Nudge the selection area within the pan/crop dialog using the up, down, left, and right arrow keys.

Position the selection box within the video frame as needed.

To rotate an event, position the mouse pointer slightly above any edge handle. The cursor changes to a looping arrow.

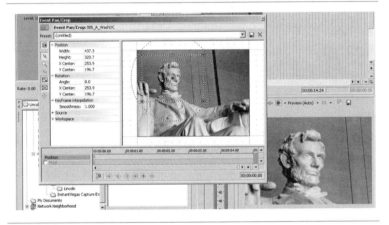

Click and drag in either direction to rotate the video image.

To reverse/flip an event, either horizontally or vertically, right-click and choose either Flip Horizontal and Flip Vertical respectively. Notice that the letter F is backwards. The letter F indicates Focus.

You can also enter values directly into the Properties settings.

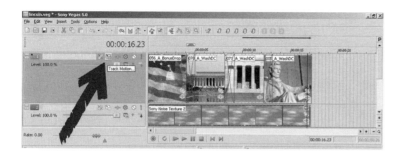

Picture-in-Picture Effects

The alternative to cropping an event is to make the whole event (or part of an event) smaller. This technique allows having more that one event displayed.

Track motion settings are fully keyframable.

Select a video track and click the Track Motion button.

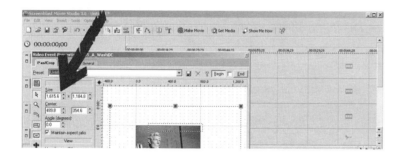

Movie Studio Users: Track motion is not supported as described here. There is a workaround, though. Use Event pan/crop as discussed above. Enter larger numbers in the size box to "shrink" the image. For example, 1440 makes the DV video one-quarter size. Position the smaller event as needed. Use Begin/End keyframes to animate the effect.

The Track Motion dialog displays. Once again there is a selection box. Video events do not show here because track motion applies to all track events. Use the Preview window to monitor your work.

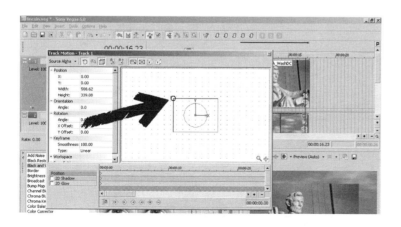

Position the cursor at any corner of the selection box, click and drag to resize.

Move the selection box to a different position, too. Nudge this using the up, down, left, and right arrow keys.

Click and drag either the Y or X to rotate the picture-in-picture effect.

Click the 2-D Shadow check box to apply a shadow; click the 2-D Glow check box to apply a glow. Control the look of these using the Properties settings or the selection area.

Track Motion is the key to Vegas 5 3D effects discussed later in this book.

To animate Track Motion, create a picture-in-picture effect as described above and leave the Track Motion dialog open.

Enable Sync to cursor to correlate the keyframe Timeline with the main Vegas Timeline.

Make sure you are at the first keyframe. Drag the selection off screen right.

Go to the end of the keyframe Timeline and drag the selection off screen left.

Close the Track Motion dialog and preview the project. The picture animates across the screen right to left. Adjust keyframes as needed to get the effect desired.

This example uses three tracks, each with separate video events. The top two clips were resized (320×240) and positioned using Track Motion. The third clip shows through underneath.

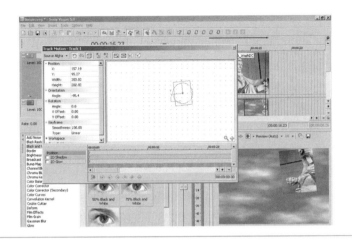

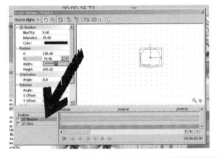

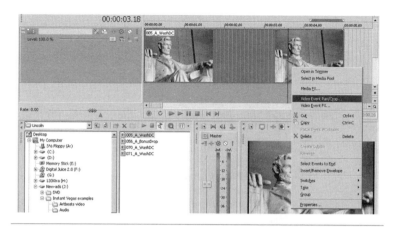

Adding Motion to Stills

Another use of Event Pan/Crop is to emulate the popular documentary look of zooming and panning on photos. This is often referred to as the Ken Burns effect.

Drag and drop a still photo on the Timeline.

Select it and click the Event Pan/Crop button.

Position the cursor at the end of the Event Pan/Crop Timeline.

Movie Studio Users: Select the End button in the dialog box.

Click an edge handle of the selection box and drag in, or crop the image somewhat.

Play the Timeline too see the picture zoom.

If the photo doesn't match the aspect ratio of your project, black bands may appear on the sides, top, or bottom. You may leave them in place or you can quickly crop the picture to fill the screen.

Set the default duration of stills using Options> Preferences Editing tab and enter a value for New still image length (seconds).

Keyframe pan, zoom, and rotation and give the illusion of motion to still images.

If a picture is sideways, rotate the image using Event Pan/Crop to the proper perspective.

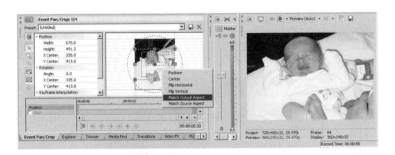

Right-click the still in the Event Pan/ Crop dialog and choose Match Output Aspect to automatically adjust to fit. Make any necessary adjustments.

The free Aspect Ratio script will quickly match all stills on the Timeline to the output aspect ratio with one click. Download this indispensable Vegas utility from www.vasst. com/login.htm.

Sometimes adding motion to photos as described can introduce some jitter, or interlace flicker when the project plays on TV. To avoid this, right-click the photo and choose Properties from the pop-up menu. Check the Reduce interlace flicker in the dialog box that displays. You may also access this via the Switches menu option found in the right-click pop-up menu.

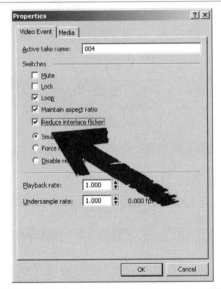

We suggest avoiding high-resolution pictures as they are more prone to interlace issues. Occasionally, adding a slight .001 blur to very high-resolution images will fix this jitter. Drag and drop the Linear Blur effect from the Video FX tab of the window docking area. This is very useful if you've taken digital images straight from your high-resolution still camera.

Set the amount to 0.001.

Movie Studio Users: Use Quick Blur instead, but try a slightly higher setting of 0.003.

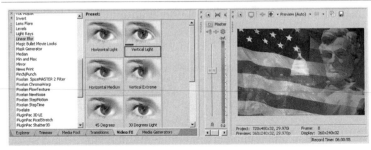

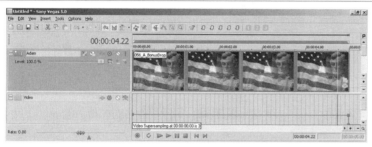

Instead of using Reduce interlace flicker, try using a super sampling envelope set to 3 or 4 during the motion on stills sequence.

Type Ctrl+Shift+B to display the main video bus track.

Right-click and choose Insert/Remove Envelope.

Add points and bring the envelope up to 3 or 4 only during the stills sequence. Take it back out when the photo montage ends.

You can also add a motion blur envelope in the same way. Motion blur makes pans, zooms, title fly-ins, fly-outs, and other animation look more natural.

Movie Studio Users: Video super sampling and motion blur are not available.

Superimposing, Levels, Opacity

Combine multiple video events through opacity. Essentially, make a top track semi-transparent, and the bottom track shows through. The two tracks superimpose like a dissolve that reaches halfway but never finishes.

Start with two events on two separate video tracks. Click and drag the top track's Level slider. Lower numbers mean more transparency. The tracks combine in a ghosting effect.

Alternately, adjust any event's opacity level by hovering near the top of the event until the icon changes to a pointing hand. Click and drag down to reduce opacity (increase transparency).

Movie Studio Users: In the absence of a track level opacity control, click the top of an event and drag down the event's opacity instead.

Adjust levels over time using an envelope. Right-click the video track header and choose Insert/Remove Envelope> Composite Level.

Add points and adjust for the desired look.

Level envelopes are a handy way to switch between tracks in a multi-camera shoot. After aligning the video events, use envelopes to dissolve (or cut) between shots.

Movie Studio Users: There are no Composite Level envelope or Automation controls.

Turn on Show Automation Controls> Automation Write (Latch), play the project, and start moving the slider. Vegas draws the envelope as you adjust the settings in real time. This can also be controlled from a MIDI device or the Mackie Universal Controller.

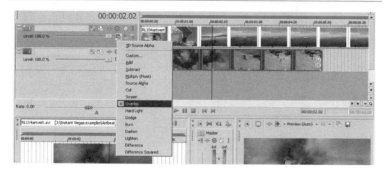

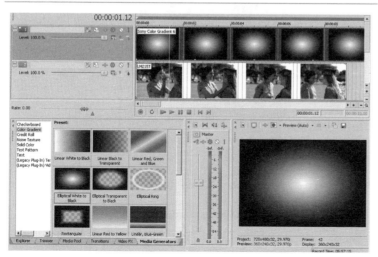

Composite Modes

Vegas includes a bevy of compositing tools that lend themselves to many creative effects. Composite modes are one tool to control track transparency. The different settings determine how much of a lower track shows through.

Movie Studio Users: There are no compositing modes available.

Click the Compositing Mode button in the track header.

Choose a compositing mode from the pop-up menu. Source Alpha is the default.

Experiment with the different modes to see how they work with your video.

Composite Using Mattes

Use mattes in conjunction with compositing modes for another unique look. Mattes are black and white (or grayscale) images, usually comprising shapes and textures.

Create two video tracks and place an event on the bottom track.

Switch to the Media Generators tab in the window docking area. Select Color gradient from the left pane and then

Search Vegas Help for "Compositing Video" to see a full-color example of how the modes operate.

Source Alpha uses alpha (transparent) channel information to determine transparency. If there isn't an alpha channel present, there is no transparency; the event is 100 percent opaque.

Create masks in your favorite image-editing software.

click and drag the Elliptical White to Black preset to the upper track.

Click the Compositing Mode button on the top track only and choose Multiply (Mask).

Preview the effect.

Composite Using Chroma Key

Chroma Key (color mask) is a way to remove a specific color and replace it with something else. For example, shoot a subject in front of a green screen and replace the green with a suitable background, such as a weather map. You can emulate this special effect, too.

First, shoot your subject against a well-lit green background. We recommend the Photoflex FlexDrop 2 portable background. It comes green on one side and blue on the reverse. Use green if shooting with digital video, and blue if shooting analog video.

Capture the footage and drop it on the Timeline. Place the background footage on the Timeline, one track lower.

Switch to the Video FX tab in the window docking area, navigate to

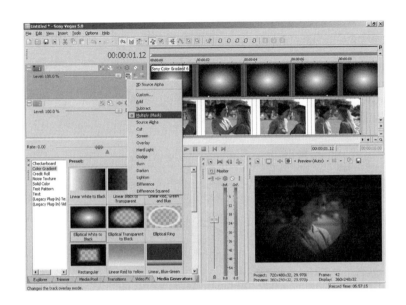

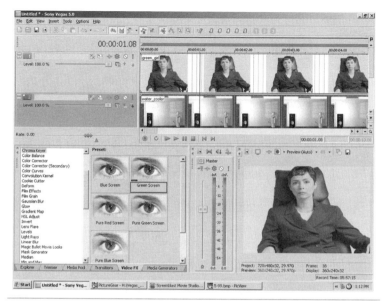

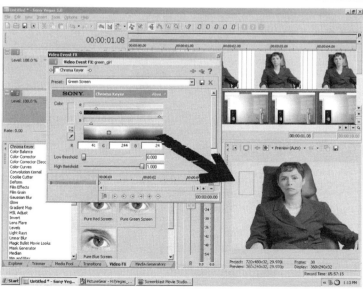

the Chroma Keyer FX, and choose the Green Screen preset.

Drag and drop the FX on the top track (the one with the subject against the green screen).

The Chroma Keyer dialog displays.

Turn off the effect for a moment by unchecking the box inside the effect's button. Click the Pick Color from Screen tool (the eyedropper).

Click and drag it over the green portion in the Preview windows. This sets the key color to the exact shade of green from your footage.

Turn the Chroma Key effect back on. The composite should look better.

For further fine-tuning, click the Show Mask only check box.

The Preview window shows only the mask generated by the effect.

Use the Low threshold and High threshold sliders to adjust the effect until the subject is pure white and the surrounding green screen area is deep black.

Remove the check from the Show mask only check box and the composite should look perfect.

For a cool "ghosting" effect, keep the Show Mask only checked and adjust for the look.

Green is the best key color to use for digital video. Make sure you light the green screen evenly (avoid shadows and hot spots). Keep the subject's shadow off the screen and prevent the green light from spilling on the subject. Also, match the lighting of the replacement background. See www.vasst.com for more tutorials on how to shoot for green screen work.

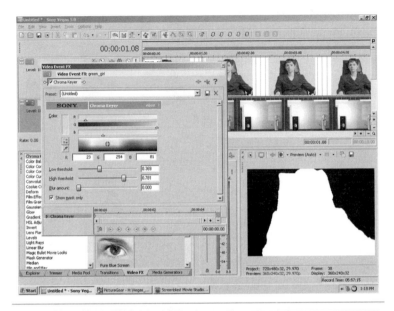

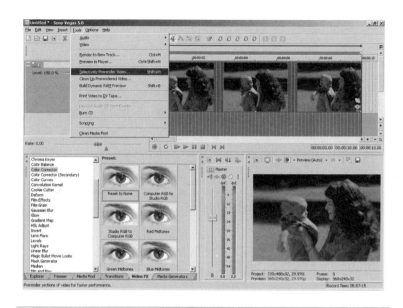

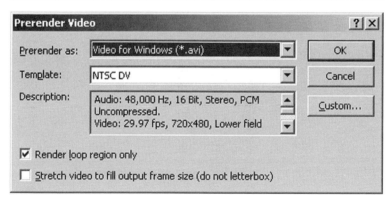

Improve Playback Performance

As projects get more complicated, you may notice that the Preview window doesn't play at the full frame rate.

Vegas and Vegas Movie Studio are designed to run without special computer hardware. As a consequence, it sometimes has to slow the frame rate down and skip frames to keep the video and audio in sync. This *only* affects real-time playback; frames will *not* be skipped during final render!

To see a complicated sequence at the full project frame rate in real time, consider rendering the section in one of two ways.

- Selectively Prerender—renders the time region to the specified format. Vegas stores this prerender until you close the project.

- Dynamic RAM Preview—renders the time selection into RAM. Vegas stores this until you initiate another RAM render. This is Douglas' favorite method of rendering small sections of video.

Make a time selection around the sequence to prerender. Click

Tools>Selectively Prerender Video or use the Shift+M shortcut.

Accept the dialog box parameters that display (they match Project Properties) or make adjustments and click OK.

When the prerender finishes, a bar appears across the Timeline shows the prerendered section. It will play at the full frame rate.

More convenient is to use the Dynamic RAM Preview. Make a time selection and choose either Tools>Build Dynamic RAM Preview or press Shift+B. The software renders the selection into RAM. This section will play at the full frame rate. If you use this feature, more RAM is obviously better.

Leave the Preview window set to a quality of Preview/Auto if you are viewing media on a computer screen. If you have connected an external monitor/television, leave the Preview setting at Preview/Full.

Set the amount of RAM to be used in Dynamic Ram Previews in Options>Preferences>Video. Go ahead and use all available RAM unless you are using other graphic-intensive applications while using Vegas.

Place a time selection around a sequence, turn on Loop Playback, and then play the section. Each iteration through the loop will move closer to the full frame rate until it's reached.

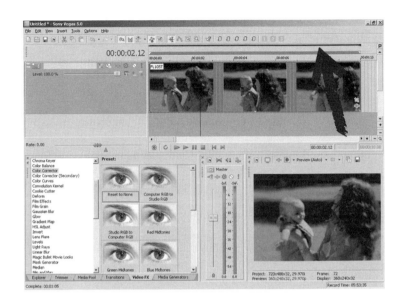

Chapter 6

Titling Tools and Video Vexations

Let's explore both the available titling functions and ways to fix less-than-perfect video quality.

Basic Titles

Both Vegas and Screenblast Movie Studio provide several built-in media generators: colors, gradients, test patterns, and text. Switch to the Media Generators tab in the window docking area and scroll through the options.

To insert a title on a video track, select Text from the left pane, then drag and drop Default Text to the Timeline. Set the default duration in Options>Preferences>Editing tab. Of course, you can extend the title as needed.

Use the Text and Backdrops tab in the window docking area.

If you draw a time selection before adding a title, its duration will be the selected length.

Movie Studio Users: Use the Text and Backdrops tab in the window docking area.

Alternately, select a track and then right-click in the Timeline and choose Insert Text Media from the pop-up menu.

Movie Studio Users: Text default duration is fixed at 10 seconds and stills are preset at five seconds. You can change title duration on the Timeline.

The Video Media Generator: Sony Text dialog box displays. There are four tabs.

• Edit—picks the font, size, bold, italics, and left, center, right justification. It's also where you type the text. You can mix and match fonts, sizes, and so forth by selecting text and setting its font and size.

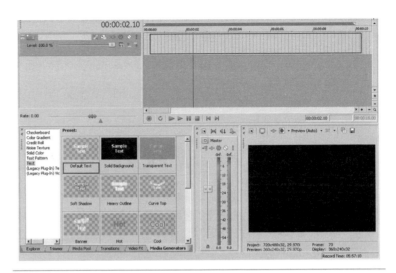

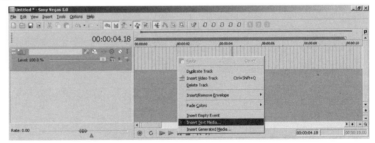

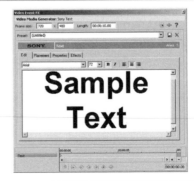

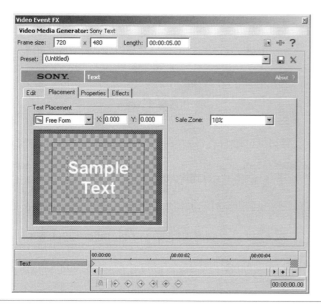

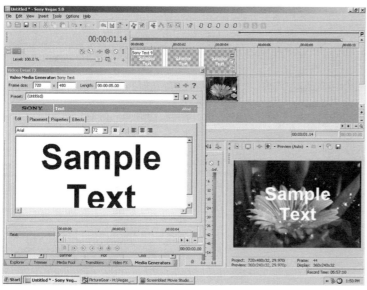

- Placement—positions the text on the screen. Click and drag the title into position. Click the drop-down box and choose from the list for preset locations. You can also use arrow keys to move the title around in the Placement window.

Projects destined for TV playback must use legal colors. Keep color values between 16 and 235 (defaults range between 0 and 255).

- Properties—adjusts text and background colors along with tracking, leading, and scaling. These settings are global for the entire text event. They apply to *all* text entered via the Edit tab.

Text settings can be keyframed and animated, too.

- Effects—sets outline, shadow, and deformation options. These, too, are global effects for all text entered in this event.

Note that the text on the Timeline has a grayscale checkerboard pattern. This indicates alpha channel information; the text has a transparent background.

If you place the text above a track with video on it, the title automatically superimposes over the video.

To edit text already on the Timeline, click the text event's Generated Media button, or right-click the text and choose Edit Generated Media.

Movie Studio Users: Click the FX button to reopen the text dialog.

Text are events and can therefore be treated with pan/crop, FX, and transitions, just as any other event.

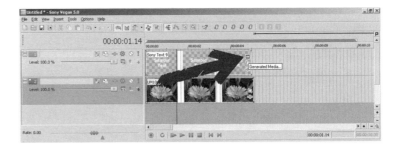

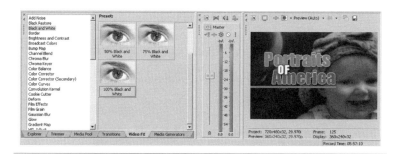

For unique looks, consider stacking multiple text tracks with different settings.

For the best legibility, use sans serif fonts, such as Arial and Impact, and keep them big and bold.

Fonts with small serifs can be hard to read and may also look jittery because of video interlacing.

Create titles in other graphics programs and save to the PNG format to retain their alpha channel information on the Timeline.

Flashy Titles

Both Vegas and Vegas Movie Studio can import Flash™ files to the Timeline for titles or special effects. Douglas uses Swish to generate his titles for Vegas, www.swishzone.com will get you to their web site where you can download a free demo.

Flash files must be Flash 5 or older in format. Flash MX files will not open in Vegas 5 or Vegas Movie Studio.

Stay Title-Safe

If your project will play on a standard TV, it's crucial to keep titles away from the edges. TVs often crop, or cut off, the extreme edges. To avoid this, place titles inside an area that is 10 to 20 percent in from the screen edge.

On the Placement tab of the text dialog box, there is a red border that indicates the title-safe area as set by the adjacent Safe Zone drop-down list.

Additionally, click the Vegas Preview window Overlay button. This applies the default Safe Areas overlay.

- Action-safe is the outer dashed line. Keep important action within this frame, which is 10 percent in from the screen edge.

Try creating Flash files with white text and use various compositing modes in Vegas to create unique title looks.

If your project will play *only* on computer, you may ignore title-safe guidelines.

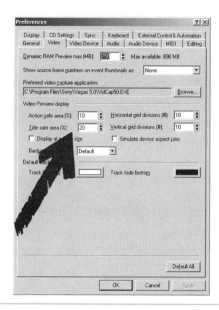

- Title-safe is the inner dashed line. Keep titles inside this box that is 20 percent in from the edge.

Set different safe area percentages using Options>Preferences>Video Tab.

Click the drop-down list box in the video Preview to select other Overlay options.

Movie Studio Users: Since there are no overlays available in the Preview window, use the Safe Zone indicator on the Placement tab in the Text/Backdrop Video Event Properties dialog.

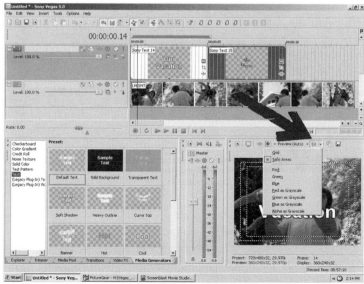

Add Text One Letter or Line at a Time

Add a text media event as described earlier. The dialog displays.

Type the first letter or line. Enter spaces for the remaining letters (or Enter for the remaining lines).

Move along the keyframe Timeline the amount of time desired before the second letter or line appears. Type the second letter or line. A keyframe gets created automatically.

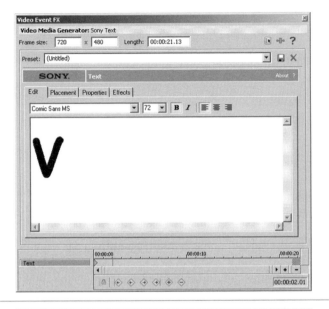

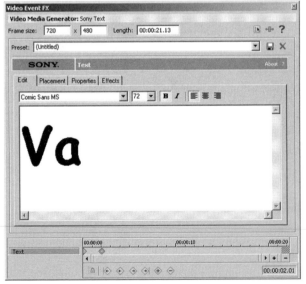

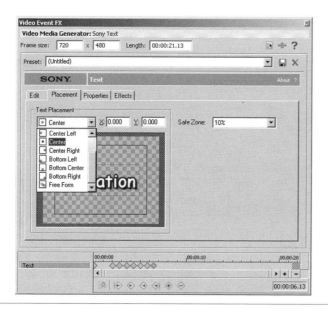

Continue as needed repeating the same steps.

Switch to the Placement tab and make adjustments. Likewise for Properties and Effects. These can be changed over time using keyframes.

Close the dialog box and preview the result.

Movie Studio Users: Because there is only begin and end keyframes, this subtle effect is not possible. Try the checkerboard technique.

Instead, arrange multiple text events and checkerboard them on multiple tracks. Transition between the events to add letters or lines as needed. This effect can be more subtle.

Gently Animate the Text

A popular look is to have text either spread out or compress slightly while on screen. It's a subtle (or not so subtle effect) that adds some motion to an otherwise static shot.

Add a text event and get the basic look you want. Switch to the Properties tab. Add a keyframe to the end.

Movie Studio Users: Press the End button.

At this last keyframe, adjust the Tracking slider to 1.2 (or more) to expand the text; less than 1 to compress.

Preview the text event and watch how it either expands or contracts as it plays.

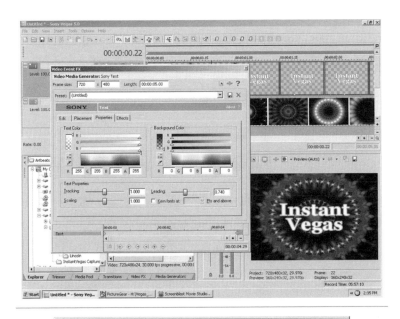

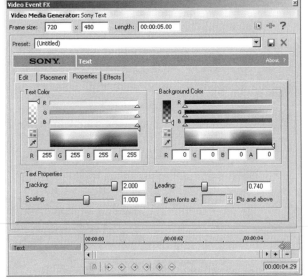

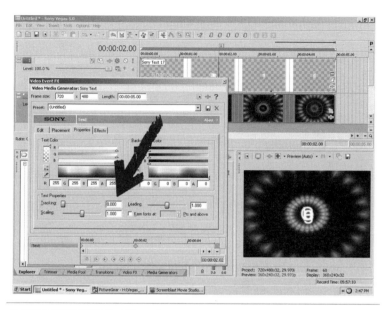

Squish the text and change it at the same time, too. Add a text event and get the basic look you want. Add a keyframe about halfway through the event and change the text. Switch to the Properties tab and pull the tracking at this keyframe all the way to the left at zero.

Create a keyframe at the end and move the tracking back to 1.0

Preview the text crushing in on itself then pulling back apart with new text. Adjust the keyframes to smooth the look (try Smooth in the middle key-frame).

Don't use scaling and keyframes to change or zoom the size of text. It will often be jumpy. Use Track Motion to zoom a title over time.

The Glow Video FX can give a similar look (or add to this one). Add it to the same text event and change from no glow to full glow and back again using three keyframes. Align the glow middle keyframe with the text change keyframe to synchronize the effects. Try Gaussian blur, too.

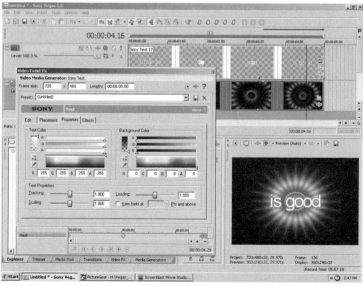

Roll the Credits

Click the Media Generators tab in the window docking area and select Credit Roll in the left pane. Drag the Scrolling on Transparent preset to the Timeline.

Double-click any slider to return it to its default value.

The Video Media Generator: Sony Credit Roll dialog box displays. Enter text in the left pane. Change properties on the right.

Movie Studio Users: The Media Generators tab is called Text and Backdrops.

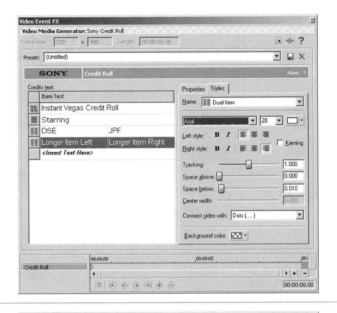

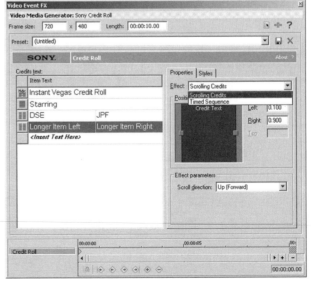

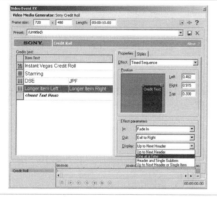

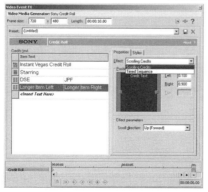

In place already are sample text and styles. Double-click to edit them. To add a line, double-click Insert Text Here and type.

Click the Style Selection to apply a style to the line.

Under Properties, choose the effect, Scrolling Credit or Timed Sequence, from the drop-down list.

For scrolling credits, adjust the Position and Scroll Direction.

For Timed Sequence, adjust the position and effects parameters.

- In—choose an entry transition.

- Out—choose an exit transition.

- Display—indicate how the text appears on screen.

Click the Styles tab to change the style look. Choose a style name from the drop-down list to change its parameters.

When complete, preview the credits.

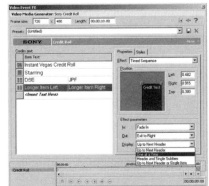

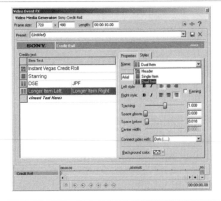

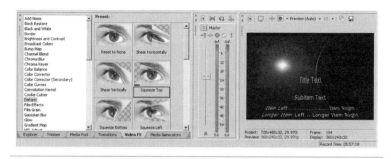

The Star Wars Look

Create a credit roll as described above. Switch to the Video FX tab in the window docking area and navigate to the Deform plug-in. Hold Shift, drag the Squeeze Top preset, and drop it on the credit roll event.

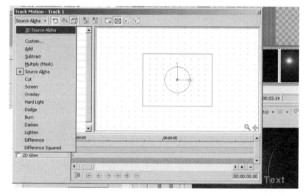

Vegas 5 users can use 3D motion instead of Deform. Click the Credit Roll's Track Motion button. Click the composite mode drop-down list and choose 3D Source Alpha.

In the Perspective box, hover over the Y, click, and drag up to position the text. Eyeball Preview as you adjust. Also, make sure your keyframe is the first and only keyframe. Close the dialog.

Don't use small fonts that contain fine lines or serifs. These create interlacing problems on most television displays. Use solid or bold fonts for best results. If the credit roll contains artifacts, consider using the Blur filter set to .001 or the Unsharp Mask filter set to Light.

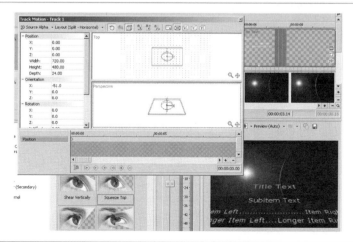

Add a track above the credit roll. Switch to the Media Generators tab, navigate to Color Gradient, and select the Linear Black to Transparent preset. Drag and drop this in the track directly above the credit roll.

In the dialog box, enter 90 for Aspect Ratio Angle.

Click the white + sign in the Control Points box. Then, type 0.444 as the Control Points Properties Y value. You can click and drag the + sign up, too. Close the dialog box.

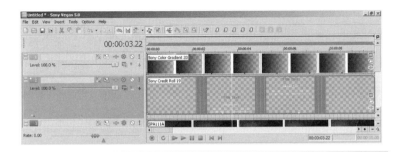

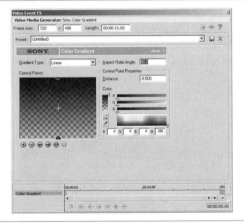

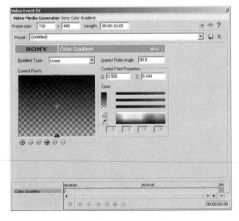

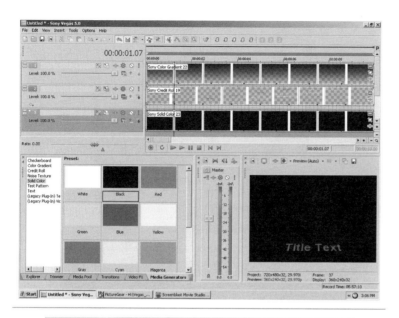

To make a star field, create a third track below the other two. Hold Shift and drag and drop the Black preset from Media Generators Solid Color.

Switch to the Video FX tab, select Add Noise, and drop the Grainy Preset on the solid black event. Adjust the Noise level to about 0.235 and uncheck Animate. Close the dialog box.

Preview your very recognizable credit roll. Fanfare anyone?

Make a Title Transparent

Add text media to the Timeline. In the dialog, switch to the Properties tab and drag the Text color slider all the way down: Alpha 0.00%.

Switch to the Effects tab and check the Draw Outline check box.

Adjust the outline color using the drop-down color picker.

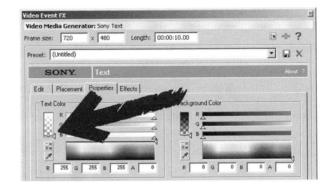

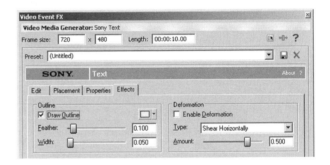

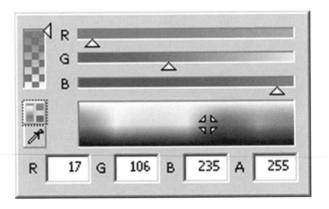

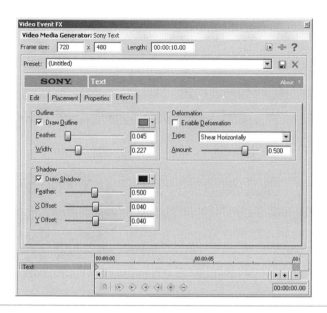

Adjust feather and width until satisfied. Shadow and deformation optional.

Note in the Preview how the video shows through the title.

Add the Light Rays Video FX to this transparent text event for interesting effects.

Fill a Title with Moving Video

Although you can create many effects using just the title generators along with Transitions and Video FX, one unique look places moving video inside a title.

Create a title following the above steps and place it on the top track. Place a video event in the track directly below this title. At this point the title superimposes, or keys, over the video.

Click the title track's Compositing mode button and choose Multiply (Mask) from the pop-up menu list. Notice the video inside the text.

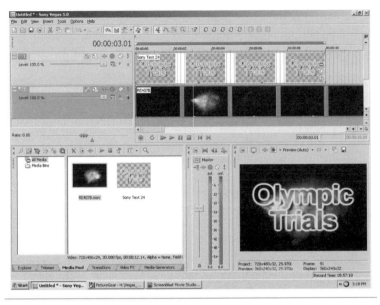

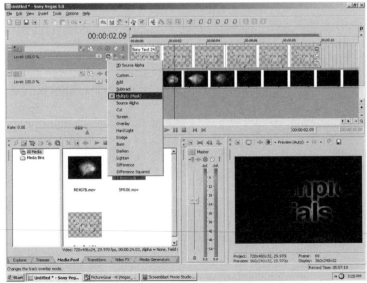

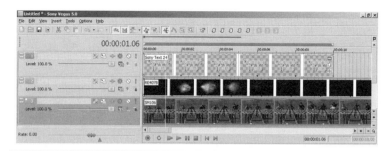

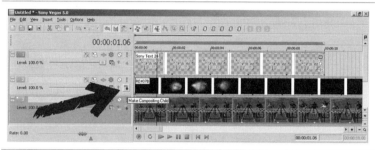

Create a third video track underneath the previous two and place video event on it.

Click track's two Make Composting Child button.

Now the title, complete with motion inside it, keys over the video.

Movie Studio Users: This look is not possible to create.

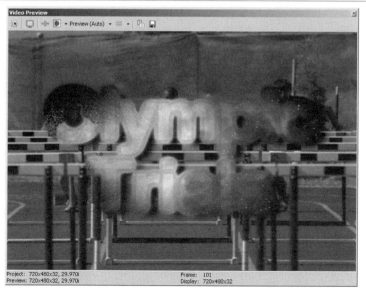

Create a Lower-Third Graphic in Vegas

Titles that extend across the bottom of the screen, called lower thirds, are useful to convey names, locations, and other information. These are also sometimes referred to as "Name Boards" or just "Boards."

Create three video tracks and place the main video on the lowest track.

Click the Media Generators tab, select color gradient, and then drag the Linear Red, Green and Blue preset to track two on the Timeline.

The Video Media Generator: Sony Color Gradient dialog displays. Adjust the look to taste and close the dialog down.

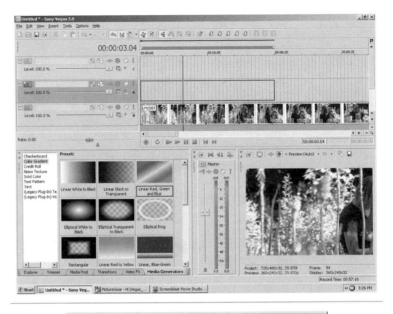

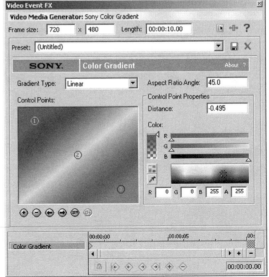

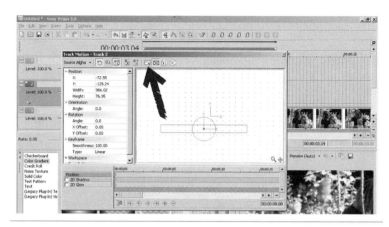

Select the Track Motion tab on the second track (with the color gradient). Turn off the Lock Aspect Ratio button in the dialog. Make sure you are at the first keyframe. Resize the track and position it accordingly.

Double-click the color gradient to create a time selection. Right-click in the track above this one and choose Insert Text Media to add a title.

In the text dialog, type and resize the text using the Edit tab.

Use keyframes and change the color gradient during its duration for an animated lower-third look.

Position the Track Motion dialog and Preview window so you can see them both.

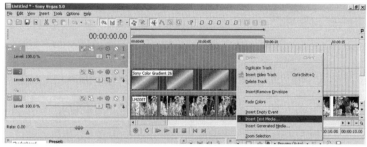

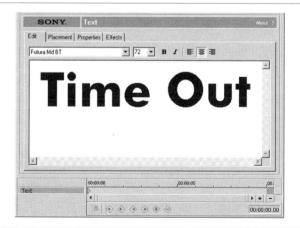

Click the Placement tab and drag the title into position using the Preview window to check the progress. When finished, close the dialog.

Add a fade-in to the lower-third graphic.

Select Linear Wipe from the Transitions tab and drag the Left-Right, Soft Edge preset to the fade-in. Add a simple fade-out to the end of the event.

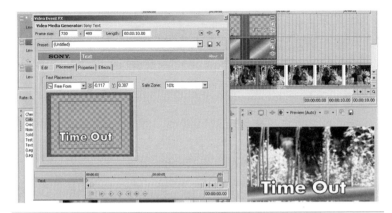

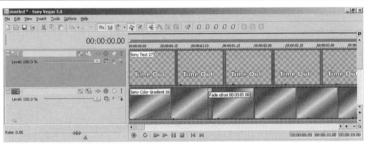

Shorten the title event and move it to the right slightly so it starts later. Add a fade-in and fade-out.

Preview the result: the lower-third graphic wipes in, the title fades in over the top, then they fade out together.

Replace the color gradient with video for motion lower thirds.

In this example, a lower-third graphic from Digital Juice replaces the color gradient as described above. No resizing or positioning was necessary, and the video has an alpha channel for keying over the video.

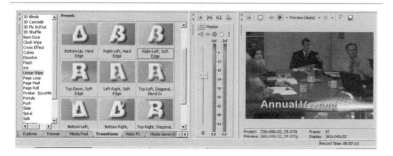

Create a Lower-Third Graphic in Screenblast Movie Studio

Click the Text and Colors tab, select Color Gradient, and drag the Linear Red, Green and Blue preset to track two on the Timeline.

The Video Event Properties Color Gradient dialog displays. Adjust the look to taste.

Switch to the Pan/Crop tab. Turn off the Lock Aspect Ratio button. Position the gradient using these settings as a starting point: Size: 575×275 and Center 300×22.

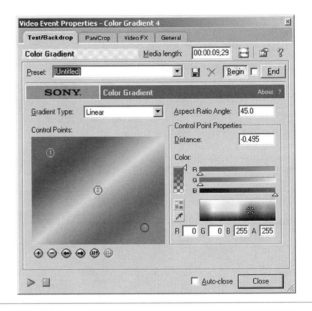

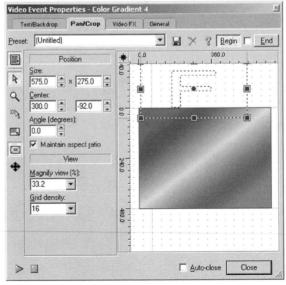

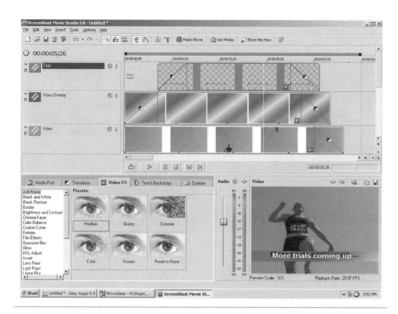

Place a title over the lower third as described in the previous section.

Add a "bug"

TV and videos often use graphics in the lower-right corner to brand their content. These icons and logos are called bugs.

Create a video track and make it the first track. This way no matter what else happens on your other video tracks, the bug is always there. Place the bug on this track and extend its duration for the project length.

Animated GIFs and moving video work well as bugs, too.

Click the Track Motion button to display the dialog. Make sure the Lock Aspect ration button is engaged. Then, resize the bug by clicking and dragging a corner of the box. Position in the lower right (mind the title safe boundaries). Add glow or shadow if desired.

Movie Studio Users: Use Event Pan/ Crop to resize and position the bug.

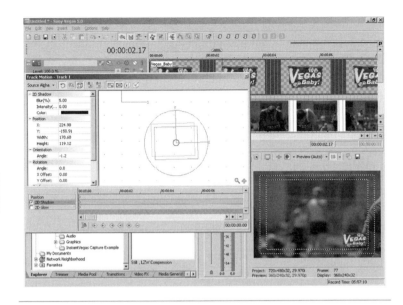

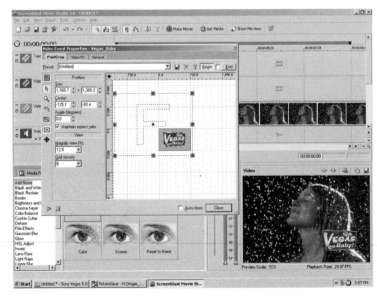

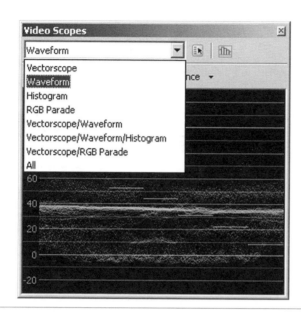

Using Video Scopes (Waveform/Vectorscope)

Vegas includes another method for looking at your video. Click View> Video Scopes to display the tools.

Choose the available scopes using from the drop-down list.

Click the Settings buttons for scope-specific options and Update Scopes while playing to have the display follow the project.

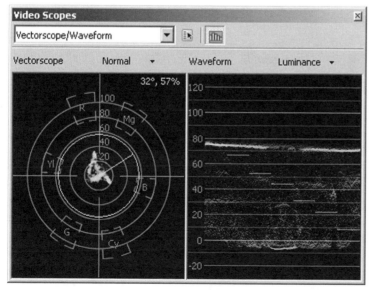

Choose the Vectorscope/Waveform combination. The scopes monitor the output after any effects in the Preview window.

Blacks should not dip below 0 and whites should not exceed 100 to be considered in range of broadcast standards.

Vectorscope—shows the color distribution and relative strength.

Waveform—shows luminance (default) strength.

Drag and drop the Broadcast Colors Conservative preset (or another option) to the Preview window to instantly force the project within broadcast standards.

Movie Studio Users: Video scopes and the Broadcast Colors FX are unavailable.

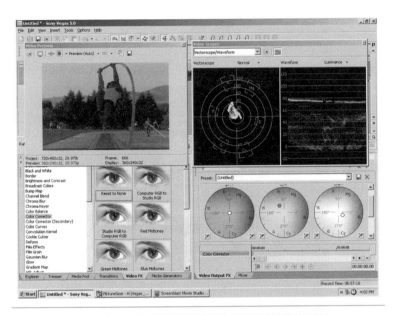

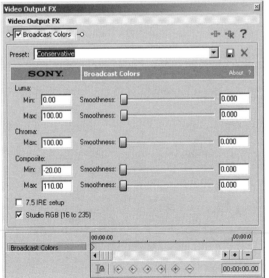

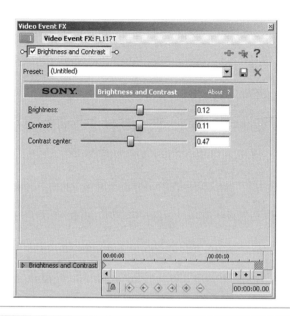

Adjust Brightness and Contrast

From the Video FX tab in the windows docking area, select Brightness and Contrast and drag it to the dark video event.

Use the sliders to adjust Brightness, Contrast, and Contrast Center or choose a preset from the drop-down list.

Monitor the before-and-after results of the effect by clicking the Split Screen View button on the Preview window.

Movie Studio Users: There is no Split Screen View available.

Simple Color Correction

Color correction is usually necessary for one of three reasons:

Use the Color Balance Video FX for additional simple color control. Douglas usually starts color correction with the Color Balance tool and then moves to the color curves control for speedy correction.

- The cameraman forgot to white balance the camera before the shoot.

- You are matching two cameras together of different models or makes.

- You are using color tools to create a specific mood.

As mentioned before, we strongly recommend that you have a reasonably good monitor or television to view color correction in real time. It's virtually impossible to accurately color correct for broadcast on a computer monitor due to differences in resolution, gamma, and color temperature.

From the Video FX tab in the windows docking area, select HSL Adjust. Drag it to a video event.

Adjust the Add to hue, Saturation, and Luminance sliders as desired. Preset looks are also available.

- Hue—selects the color to apply.

- Saturation—controls the strength of the chosen hue.

- Luminance—sets the brightness of the video.

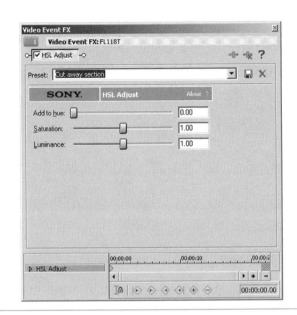

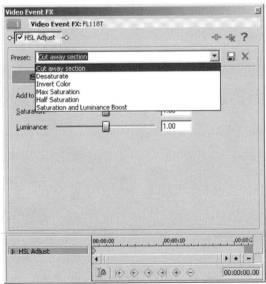

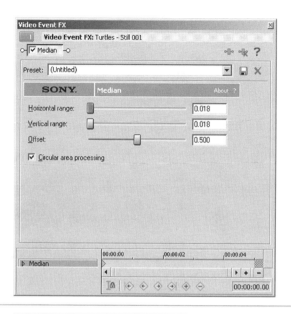

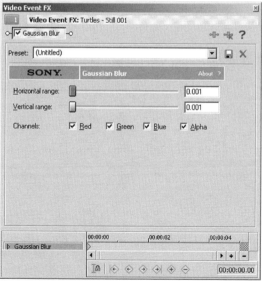

Reducing Video Noise

Sometimes video looks a little grainy, usually from low-light situations.

Drag the Median Filter>Light Noise Reduction preset to the offending events.

Check the Circular area processing check box.

Movie Studio Users: There is no Median Filter; try adding a little blur.

Sometimes Gaussian Blur with a subtle 0.001 or 0.002 setting on all channels works well at reducing video noise and grain. The Median filter should be last in any color correction or other FX chains you might create.

Fixing Blurry Video

Duplicate the blurry video event and align it above itself on the upper track.

Drag the Convolution Kernel to the top event only. Use the Sharpen Preset.

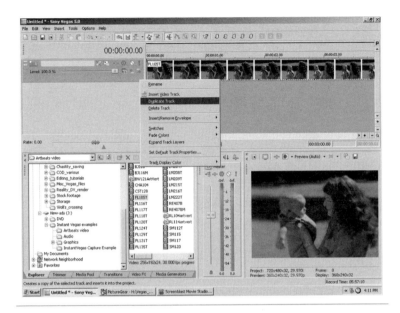

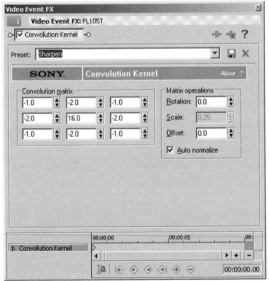

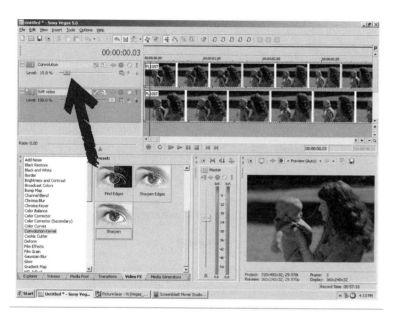

Blend the top to the bottom track by setting its opacity to 10 to 15 percent of top. Adjust to taste.

Movie Studio Users: Substitute the Convolution Kernel with the Sharpen FX to achieve a similar result.

The same technique for fixing blurry video can reduce graininess, too.

Advanced Color Correction

Movie Studio Users: These techniques apply to Vegas only. As an alternative, apply three iterations of the Color Balance Video FX. Set one for Highlights, the second for Midtones, and the third for Shadows. Adjust the sliders on each to taste.

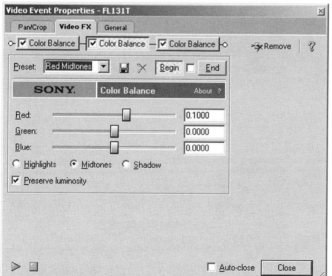

Add the Color Curves Video FX to the track or event to process.

There are a variety of presets available for certain quick looks.

The Color Curves work on the Red, Green, and Blue Channels. Select a channel and drag a point at either end to adjust.

Also, double-click a curve line to add a point. Click and drag the point to adjust.

Notice the light gray tangents around the point. Click either tangent end and drag to adjust the curve further.

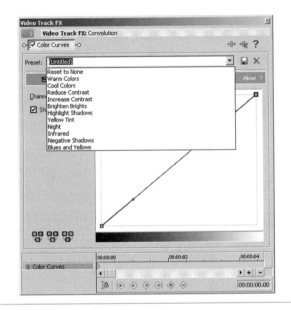

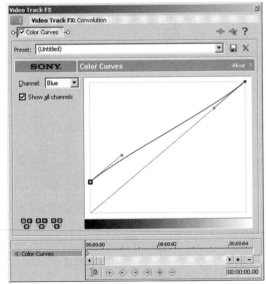

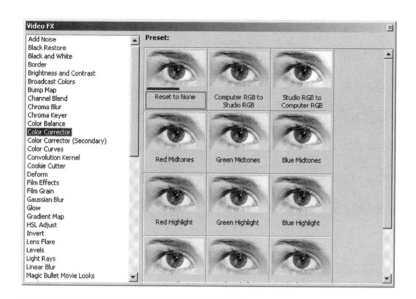

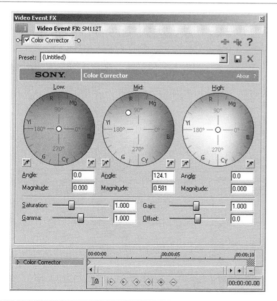

Using Three-Wheel Color Correction

Drag the Color Corrector Video FX and drop it on the track or event to process.

The Color Corrector dialog displays. Three color wheels dominate the screen along with global settings for Saturation, Gain, Gamma, and Offset.

- Low—adjusts the low or darker colors such as shadows.

- Mid—adjusts the mid colors such as skin tones.

- High—adjusts the highlight colors.

Click the white circle inside a color wheel and drag it to adjust. Move toward a color on the wheel to add it to the video. Further away from center adds more color.

Another way to use this tool is to select the color you want to add from the video itself. Position the Color Corrector dialog so the Preview window is visible.

Use the color corrector in conjunction with the video scopes.

Click the Choose Adjustment Color (+ eyedropper) tool and then select the color to add by dragging a box on the Preview window in an area with the color.

To remove a color from the video, click the Choose Complementary Color (– eyedropper) tool and drag a selection over the color to remove in the Preview window. This often yields better results.

Using Secondary Color Correction

Sometimes you either want to add or subtract a color. The single-wheel color corrector will work well. However, its real strength lies in applying color to a specific range only. For example, this effect can change the sky color *without* affecting anything else.

Drag the Color Corrector (Secondary) Video FX and drop it on the event to process. Position the dialog box to reveal the Preview window, too.

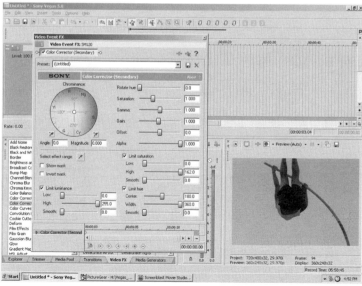

After selecting a specific color to be singled out, reduce saturation in the upper portion of the Secondary Color Correction tool to zero. Watch everything in the frame go to black and white except the color that you've singled out. Use the Luma and Saturation controls in the Secondary Color Correction tool to fine-tune the color settings.

Click the Select effect range button. Next, drag a selection box over the color or range of colors to be affected in the Preview window.

Adjust the color wheel to apply its effect to only the suggested range.

Click the Show Mask check box and adjust the Limit luminance, Limit saturation, and Limit hue sliders to fine-tune the effect. Clear the check box when finished.

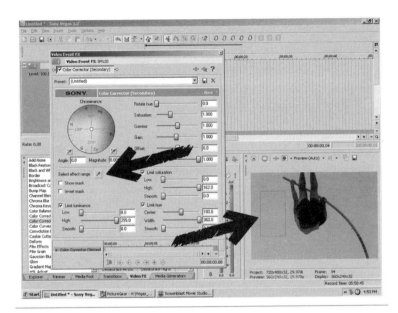

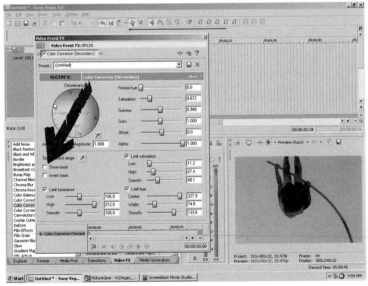

Chapter 7

Sound Off!

Both Vegas and Screenblast Movie Studio give you wide-ranging tools for making your video look great. Both tools also have extensive audio features that can make your audio sound even better. And unlike many other NLEs where audio is an afterthought, Sony's audio approach fully integrates with the video portion.

Sound Messages

Many of the tips and techniques explained so far apply to audio. Like video, audio is just another event on the Timeline. When it comes to editing, trimming, moving, crossfading, and arranging, treat audio just like video. Crossfades, fade-outs, and volume are all managed the same way as video is.

One of the great features of both programs is the ability to watch the video as you record sound. This makes recording in sync with the picture a snap.

Be sure to turn
ON Quantize to
Frames when
working with
video, OFF for
audio.

IMPORTANT: Audio is continuous, not frame-based as video. Therefore, when working with audio, either exclusively or on conjunction with video, *turn off* Quantize to Frames. Go to Options> Quantize to Frames or use the Alt+F8 shortcut.

Also, audio doesn't follow the top-down motif as-video. Consider audio as always being a composite or mix of its various contents.

All audio is available when on the Timeline, and you have several methods for controlling the mix of all your sound elements. Track levels for the overall level of each track.

• Mute and Solo buttons (mute is automatable in Vegas).

• Audio event attack, sustain, release (ASR) envelope for fading in (A), main level (R), and fading out (S). Move to the top of the audio event and drag the little pointing finger down. Move to either edge of the audio event (cursor changes to pie shape) and drag for fades. Right-click for fade choices.

• Track volume (and pan) envelope on a track to automate level over time. Vegas includes automation recording, too.

• Buses for grouping audio tracks and controlling their overall volume.

• Master bus fader for overall project level.

Many of these were discussed earlier in the book; others will be featured here.

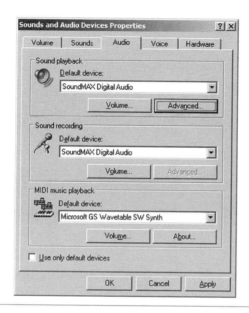

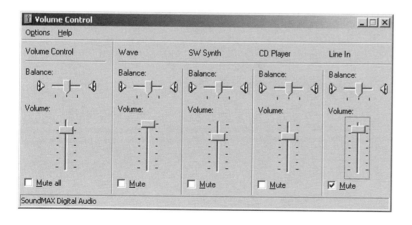

Prepare to Record

To get started recording, hook up an audio source. For example, to record a voice-over (VO), connect the mic to the sound card. If using an external mic preamp or a mixer, connect the mic to the preamp or mixer first and then its line inputs to the sound card. Refer to the instructions that came with your sound card or mixer for details about hooking up audio sources.

Some USB- and FireWire-based audio interfaces do not use separate software. Set levels on the mixer connected to it or use its on-board level controls (if available).

Set levels at the preamp or mixer and also using any software that controls the sound card. For example, access the standard Windows sound card controls from Start>Control Panel> Sounds and Audio Devices. If there is a speaker icon in the Taskbar, click it to access the same tools.

Click the Advanced tab to show the Windows volume control. The default shows the playback levels of the various sound devices connected to your computer system.

Click Options>Properties to switch to the sound card's recording settings.

Select the Recording button and click OK.

Choose the appropriate input device. In this example, click the check box under Line In and use the slider to adjust the level. Alternately, select microphone and adjust the level accordingly. Under the Advanced tab are additional microphone settings.

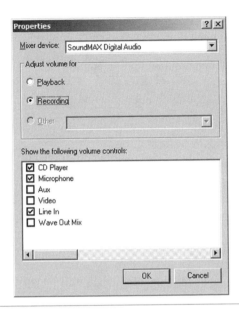

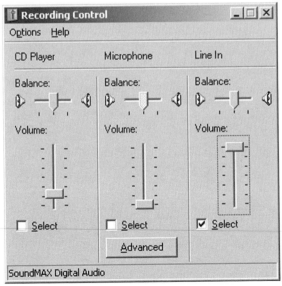

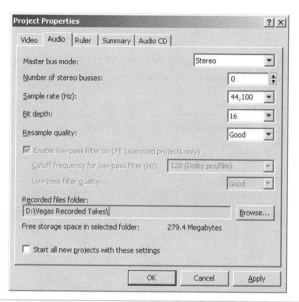

Next, set up a folder to hold your recording. Click File>Properties>Audio tab and locate or create a folder using Recorded files folders.

Movie Studio Users: Setup the record folder using File>Project Properties> Folders>Media Folder.

Insert an audio track on the Timeline and click the Arm for Record button.

Extracting audio from a CD is explained earlier in this book.

When choosing music for your production, ask these questions: What emotional response do you desire? What style is appropriate? Where will you use music specifically?

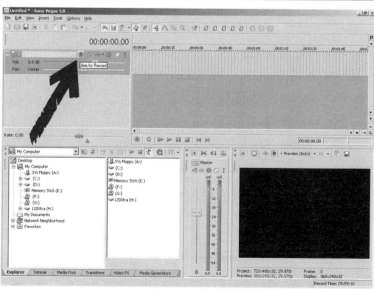

The Project Recorded Files Folder dialog box displays. Accept the default entered above or choose a new location for your recording. Click OK.

Never let your audio recording exceed zero on the meters or it will sound distorted.

Notice the meters displaying in the track. Keep your recording levels between –18 and –3 for the best results. The Volume slider controls only the playback volume of the track, not the record level. Average level should be around –6. See above for setting levels.

Movie Studio Users: There is no Arm for Record. Click the Record button on the track header to start recording immediately on the selected track at the cursor position.

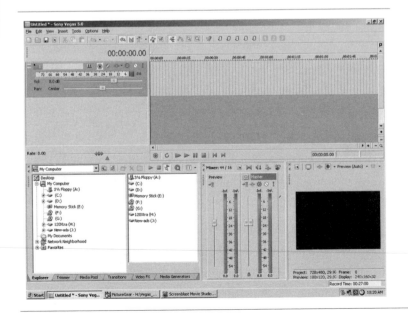

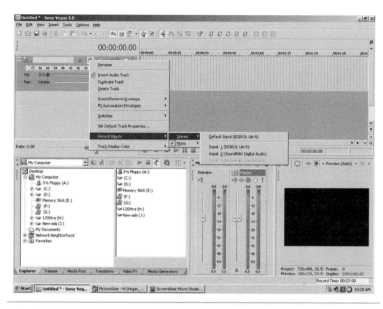

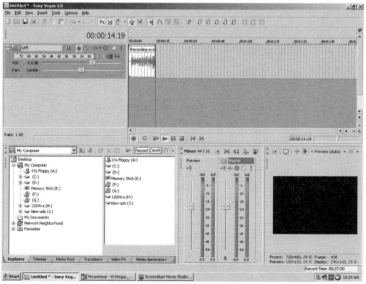

Depending on your audio hardware, you may be able to record multiple tracks simultaneously. Right-click the Arm for Record button and choose Record Inputs. Select from the available options, which vary depending on your configuration.

Insert additional tracks and assign inputs as desired.

Click the record button or use the Ctrl+R shortcut. Vegas begins recording on the selected track at the cursor position. The waveform draws on the screen, too.

When recording is complete, press Stop or Esc. The Recorded Files dialog displays. Choose from the options accordingly.

Add more tracks or position the cursor to record more audio as needed.

Because of its multitrack capabilities, Vegas is the recording software of choice for many musicians. Vegas can record up to 26 tracks simultaneously.

Record Multiple Takes

You can record additional takes into the same event, too.

Select an already recorded audio event and position the cursor. Click Arm for Record. When ready, click Record and then Stop when finished.

The new recording is added as a take. The original recording remains as another take.

Alternately, make a time selection and turn on Loop Playback. Position the cursor at the start of the loop. Start recording as described above.

This records take after take into the loop region until stopped. This is great for fixing mistakes.

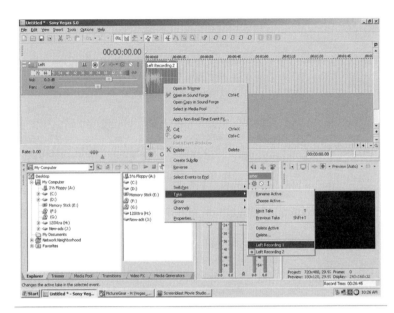

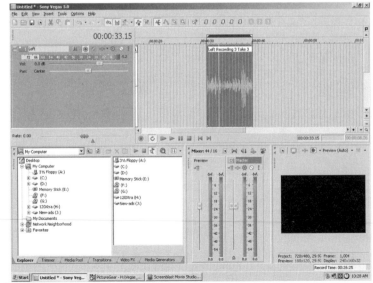

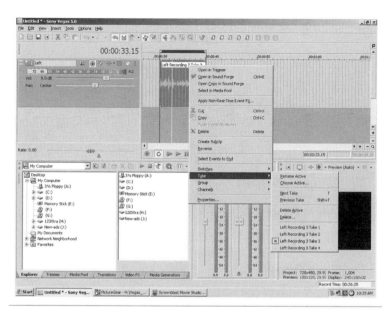

Right-click an event and scroll to Take in the pop-up menu. The information about the takes appear. Choose from the available options.

Click Choose Active to display the Take Chooser dialog, if you prefer.

Takes are a great way to audition different music choices. Right-click, drag, and drop several music tracks on top of each other choosing Add as Takes from the pop-up menu. Then, switch music takes as you watch your project.

Quickly cycle through takes on the Timeline by selecting the event containing takes and repeatedly typing the T key for the next take or Shift+T for the previous take.

Cleaning Up Production Dialog

Getting good sound on location is difficult at best. While you should strive to get the best recordings possible up front, there are a few fixes available.

Checkerboarding the voice events on adjacent tracks can make dialog smoothing easier.

One common mistake picture editors make is always cutting the audio and video in the same place. This is a simple procedure: position the cursor and press S to cut both audio and video. The problem is that audio often doesn't blend smoothly from shot to shot. Tying it to an abrupt visual statement only compounds the audio jump.

Good dialog editors overcome this problem by either cutting just before or after the picture cut or by using audio crossfades. From a workflow standpoint, you'll probably want to cut the audio and video at the same time first.

Called the J edit, cut the dialog when the person finishes speaking before the picture cuts to someone else. This brings in the next shot's audio earlier. Select the corresponding audio event, right-click it, and choose Group>Remove From to ungroup the audio from its video or use the shortcut U.

Shorten the event, being careful not to cut off any words or parts of words.

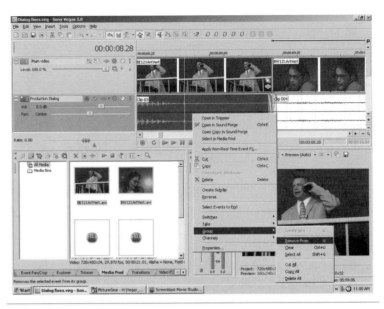

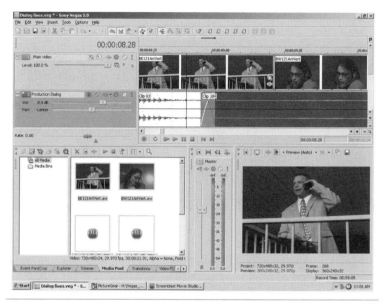

Ungroup the adjacent audio event and extend to fill the gap. A short overlap can further smooth the dialog. Make sure automatic crossfades is turned on in the Toolbar.

The keyboard shortcut Z mutes and X solos the selected track (audio and video).

To make an L cut, extend the previous cut's sound until the next person starts talking. The person's speech covers up the edit well. Select the second sound event and ungroup it from its video. Shorten it until the dialog starts. Listen carefully as you might cut off a breath.

Select the first sound event, ungroup it, and drag it out to fill the gap. Crossfades are optional.

Or use crossfades on the tracks to smooth the dialog. Remember that you have several crossfade options.

Another trick is to use room tone recorded on location to fill in the gaps and further smooth the dialog edits. The idea is to have a smooth sound, free of annoying sound jumps.

More often than not, steady noise or background sounds cover up edits best. The ear-brain combination is rather adept at tuning out the background noise and focusing on what's being said. It's when the presence jumps from shot to shot that draws attention to the problem and ruins the illusion. For example, you have wind noise in some dialog, but not all. Add wind noise recorded on location under the dialog during the whole sequence. In a pinch, you can blend wind noises from a stock library, if you carefully select wind that closely approximates the wind heard in your audio. Use EQ to more closely match sounds.

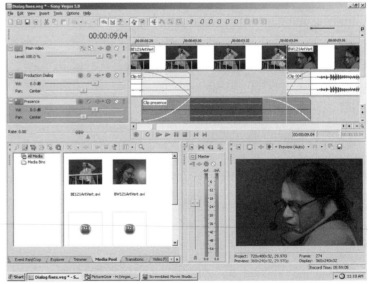

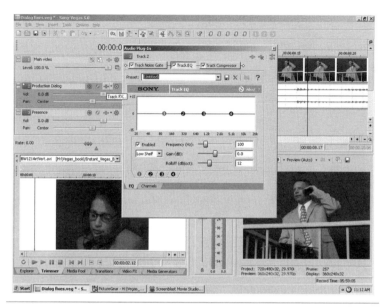

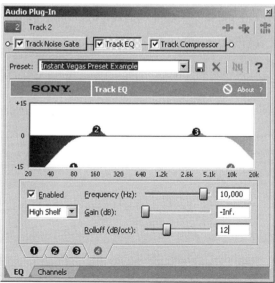

Equalization affects the tonal balance of sounds. Vegas includes the Track EQ plug-in by default on every audio channel.

Try these general settings when working with production dialog.

- Roll off the extreme lows from 80Hz down to get rid of rumble and subsonic noise. This would include micstand noise.

- Add a 2–4dB bump at 160Hz to add warmth to male voice, 320Hz for female.

- Add 2–4dB at 1.75 kHz or 3.5kHz or both for speech intelligibility. This may bring out excessive "ess" sounds, called sibilance.

- Add 2–4dB in the 6–8kHz area to add some sparkle to a dull recording.

- Reduce the muddy midrange by 2–4dB in the 500–800Hz range.

Movie Studio Users: The ExpressFX Equalization is available on each of the three audio tracks. Replace it with the ExpressFX Graphic EQ to make the above settings.

Switch to the Track Compressor and choose the 3:1 compression starting at –15dB preset to further smooth the dialog level.

Eliminating Noise

If your recording has too much room and not enough speech (caused by having the mic too far away in a large room), you may be able to fix it somewhat (it'll never be perfect, though).

Add the Paragraphic EQ to the offending track and use these settings:

- Enable and set the low-shelf to 100Hz and the amount to –inf.

- Enable and set the high-shelf to 10,000Hz and its amount to –inf, too.

- Set the first slider Gain between 4–6dB, Width to 0.7oct, and the Center frequency to 160Hz for male voice, 320Hz for female.

- Set the adjacent slider to add intelligibility to speech. Try 4–6dB, Width 1.0oct, and Center frequency at either 1,750Hz or 3,500Hz (not both).

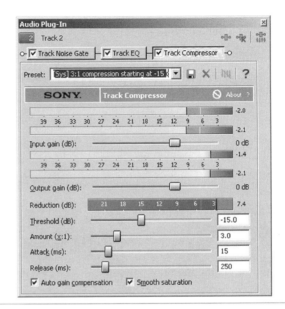

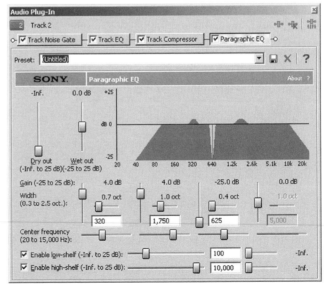

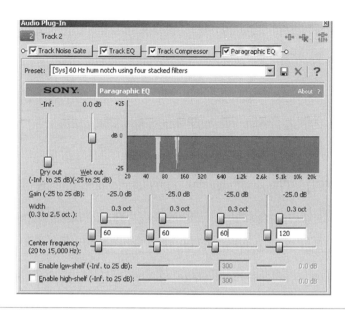

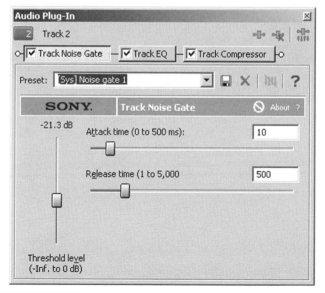

Find the sound of the room by using the third slider. Boost the gain significantly. Play the file and sweep the center frequency until the room sound is far louder. When you find the sound, turn the gain all the way down to cut out the room resonance.

Too much hum on your recording? Add the Paragraphic EQ to the humming Track FX chain. Choose the "60Hz hum notch using four stacked filters" Preset from the list. Changing one of the filters to 120Hz is more effective.

Another way to eliminate noise on a track is via the Track FX Track Noise Gate. However, this device works like a switch, essentially turning off the track to eliminate the noise when there is no dialog and turning it back on when the dialog plays. The noise will still be under the dialog but should be masked by the speech. Therefore, the constant cutting in and out of the noise may make the track sound worse, not better.

To turn off noise on a track, use the Track Noise Gate. Play the track and set the Threshold so the noise goes away. Higher settings mean more noise gets cut off, but be careful not to chop of starts and ends of words.

To scrub audio directly on the Timeline, hover the mouse over the cursor, hold Ctrl and drag left or right.

Change the default FX included on an audio or video track by clicking the Track FX button. Create the FX chain you desire and save the chain as a Preset. Close the dialog, right-click the Track Header, and select "Set Default Track Properties." Check the boxes of what to include and click OK.

Mangle Sounds in Unique Ways

As fun as many Video FX are, there are also some unique audio effects available, too.

Avoid having too many audio effects on tracks. Consider placing effects on buses or as insert FX instead.

Make a voice sound as if it's coming from a telephone by adding the Parametric EQ to the Track FX chain.

Use the "Phone line effect" preset.

Make alien and other worldly sounds by applying the Flange/Wah-Wah plug-in to the track. Go through the various presets until you find the sound you want.

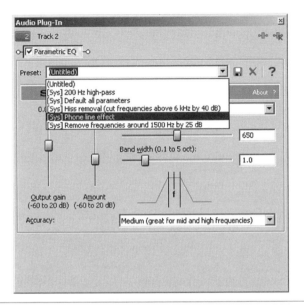

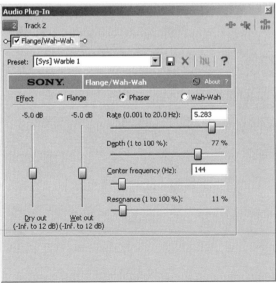

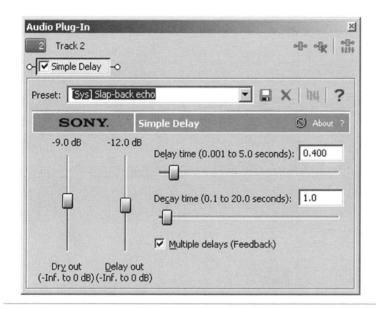

Add distinct repeats to a track using the Simple Delay plug-in. Try the "Slap-back echo" preset and engage the Multiple delays (Feedback) check box and move the slider to 1.0.

Create a variety of rooms in which to place your sounds using the Reverb plug-in. Again, presets can get you started. Season to taste.

Movie Studio Users: There are similar ExpressFX that can closely approximate these effects.

Toggle between monaural and stereo by clicking the Mixer's Downmix Output button.

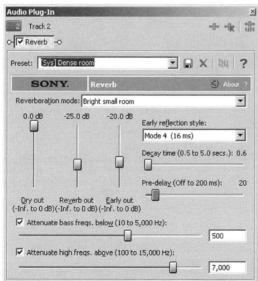

Busing in Vegas

Busing, as its name implies, is a way to move audio around in your project. Buses are great for grouping similar sounds and applying FX and volume to them all at once. Insert FX buses allow multiple tracks to share the same effect, such as one overall reverb for a music project.

Switch to the mixer window and click the Insert Bus button to add a new bus. Vegas supports 26 buses.

Buses have the same functionality as track headers: Routing, Bus FX, Automation, Mute, Solo, Pan fader, and Volume fader.

To assign a track to a bus, click its bus button and choose from the list.

The bus letter assignment displays in the track header.

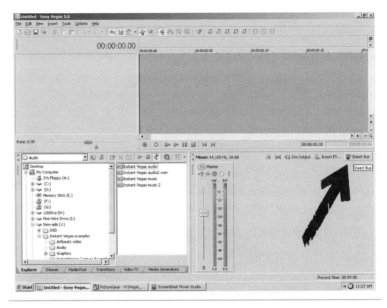

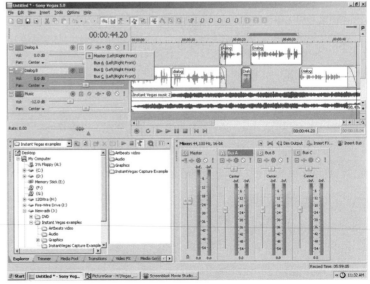

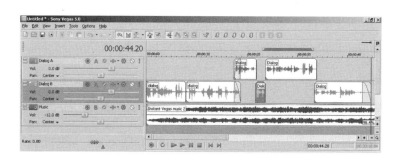

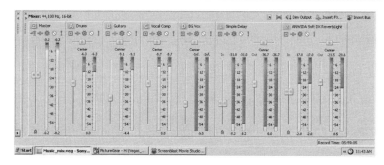

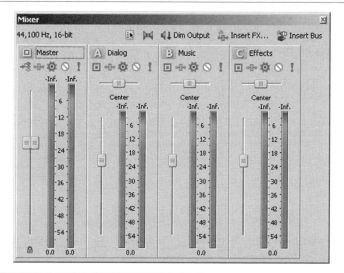

To assign the bus routing, click its bus button. The default routes the bus to the master. You can choose other routing, depending on your audio hardware configuration. Bus-to-bus routing is also available.

This example shows using buses in a music project. The drums were recorded to many separate tracks. Routing these individual tracks to one bus makes controlling the entire kit easier. The same is true for multiple guitar and vocal tracks.

For video projects, set up three buses and route all the dialog tracks to one, music to another, and sound effects to a third. This lets you control the DM&E (Dialog, Music, and Effects) balance with just three faders.

View the audio bus tracks by clicking View>Audio Bus Tracks or use the B shortcut. This duplicates the buses under the track headers. Here you can add and edit automation envelopes, too.

Insert FX are the way to route many sounds to the same audio effect, therefore saving the processor from having to work so hard. Typical insert effects include reverb and delay, especially when mixing music.

Click the Insert FX button in the Mixer window.

The Plug-in Chooser dialog box displays. Select an effect or build a chain as needed.

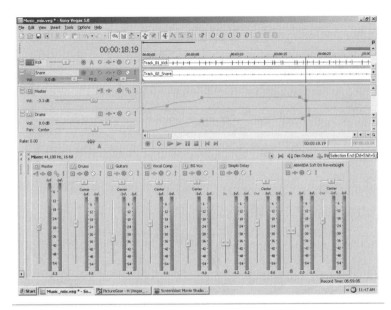

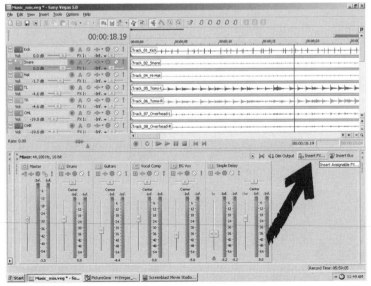

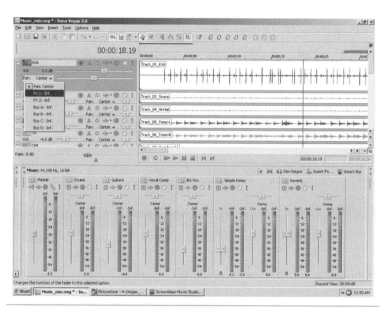

In the track header, the Pan slider is now multipurpose. Click the arrow to display the list and make the choice.

This slider now determines how much of the track gets sent to the Insert FX. It's the software equivalent of splitting the audio in two places.

Turn the Dry out to –inf to make Insert FX 100% wet. Use the Track Volume and FX level to balance to effect's Wet/Dry mix.

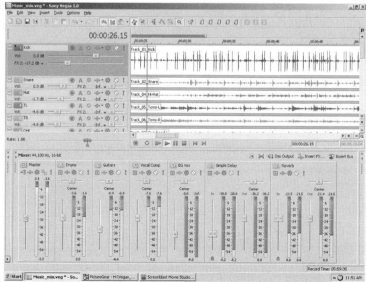

The master bus can also have effects. Click the Master FX button and choose the plug-in(s).

Try using the Wavehammer plug-in on the master and start with its Master for 16-bit Preset. This adds a gentle over-all compression to tighten up the mix.

Movie Studio Users: You can apply audio effects to the master Audio bus. Try the ExpressFX Dynamics and use its 2:1 compression preset.

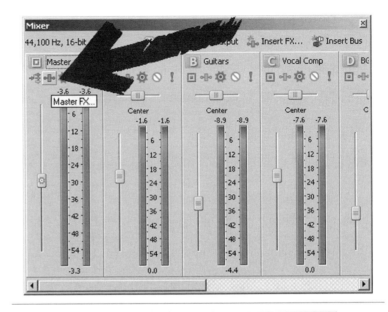

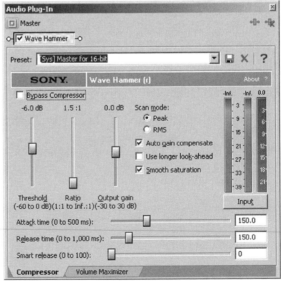

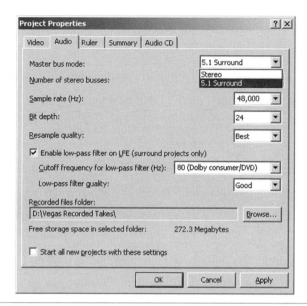

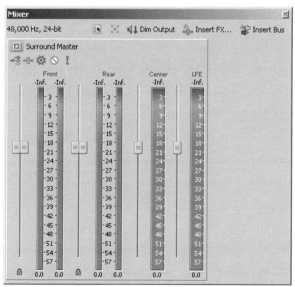

5.1 Surround Sound

Vegas fully supports mixing in 5.1 surround sound. Purchase the optional Dolby AC-3 encoder (included in Vegas+DVD-A) to render your surround mixes to AC-3 for DVD playback. Mixing in surround also requires a soun card with six discreet outputs and six powered speakers.

To change to a 5.1 project, click the Project Audio Properties button in the mixer or choose File>Properties>Audio tab. Set the master bus mode to 5.1 surround. Also, Enable low-pass filter on LFE and select 80 (Dolby consumer/ DVD) from the drop-down list.

The mixer shows meters and faders for the surround channels.

The Pan slider on audio track headers, buses, and Insert FX has been replaced by the Surround Panner. Use this to position the track, bus, or Insert FX.

Double-click a Surround Panner for a bigger display. Resize this window as needed. Obviously, the speaker icons represent the speakers. Clicking them toggles turning them on and off for the selected track, bus, or Insert FX only.

The flashing diamond represents the positioning. Click and drag it to the desired location.

Surround comprises L/R stereo, L/R surround, dedicated center, and a low-frequency enhancement channel (LFE).

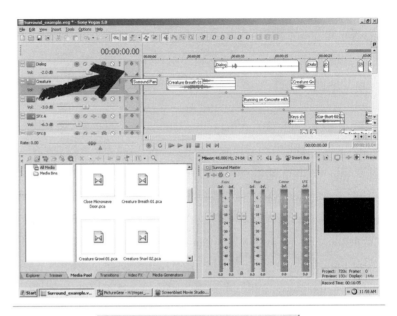

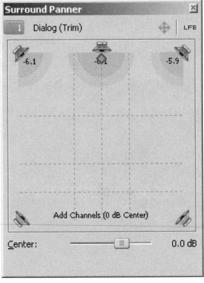

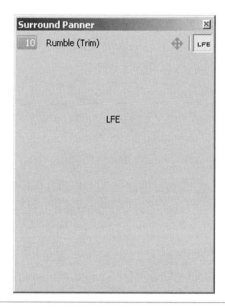

Assign to the LFE by clicking the LFE Only button in the upper-right corner.

Surround panning can be automated in two ways.

If you turn on automation controls, the diamond changes to match the automation icon. Play the project and move the positioning to automate panning over time.

Right-click the Surround Panner and choose Film from the pop-up menu to emulate film-style 5.1 mixing.

Instantly turn down the Vegas volume by clicking the Dim Output button on the Mixer. Typing Ctrl+Shift+F12 will enable dimming as well.

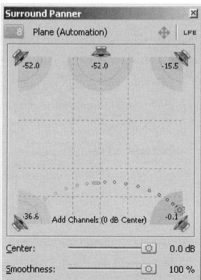

Right-click the track header and choose Insert/Remove Envelopes>Surround Pan Keyframes. Click the Expand Track Keyframes for a better view.

Adjust the Surround Panner and add keyframes as needed. The automation also adds keyframes, which you can then edit.

For more details about surround sound, see *Instant Surround Sound* also available from VASST/CMP Books.

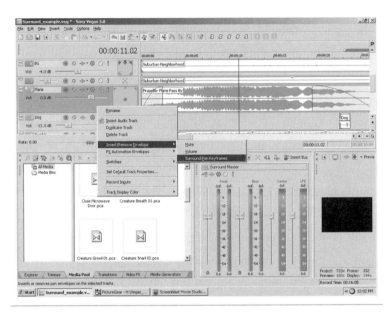

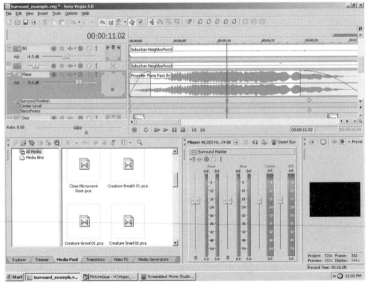

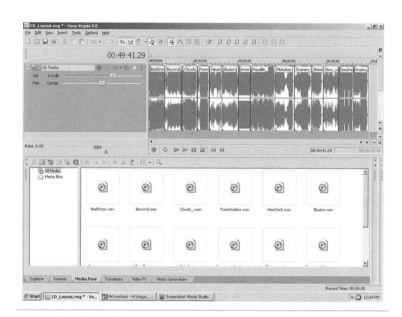

Authoring and Burning CDs

Vegas can be used as a music mastering tool and even burns RedBook-compliant CDs. First, place your final mixed music tracks on the Timeline, either on individual tracks or all on one.

Add any effects as needed. The optional Ozone plug-in (www.izotope.com) is a great-sounding, all-around mastering tool. Insert it on the master bus as a Master FX.

Leave a two-second gap at the start of the Timeline before the first track begins.

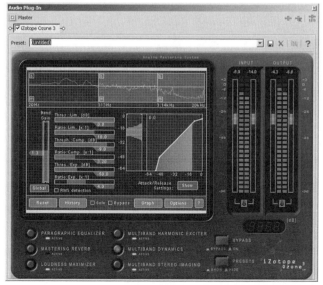

Double-click each music track to select it and type N to insert the track marker/PPQ index. Repeat this for each music track.

When complete, click Tools>Burn CD> Disc-at-Once Audio CD and follow the dialog box instructions.

Integration with Sound Forge

For more extensive audio editing chores, Vegas integrates with Sound Forge. Right-click an audio event and choose Open Copy in Sound Editor.

Use the tools in Sound Forge and then save the file.

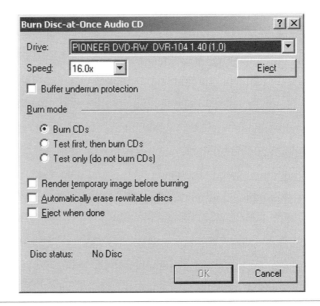

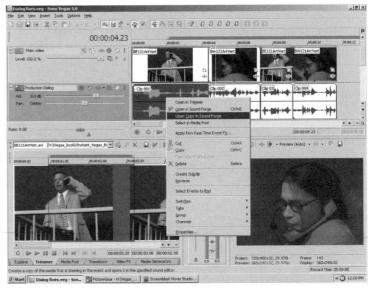

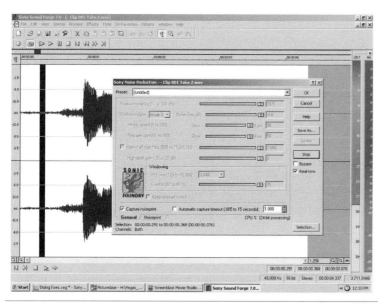

Switch to Vegas and the fixed file shows up as a take. The original file remains, too.

Movie Studio Users: You can edit and process sound files using Sound Forge Studio, too, as described earlier.

Audio for Video Secrets

Sound is 70 percent of the visual experience. Don't believe us? Turn on your favorite movie and turn off the sound. Not quite the same, is it?

Audiences will put up with "bad" video, but NEVER poor sound. Poor audio ruins the experience and immediately screams amateur! Memorable soundtracks have the power to inform, entertain, and elicit the desired emotional response. Thankfully, audio is often the easiest and cheapest way to make your video production look better and deliver the message more effectively.

Here are some basic guidelines:

- Dialog rules most productions. Focus on capturing voice in production. Other sounds can be added in post-production.

- The typical built-in camcorder microphone is good for one thing: picking up the noise of the camera. Use a separate, directional microphone. We recommend Audio Technica products.

- The best mic technique is to point the mic at the source of the sound you want and get as close as possible to it.

- Consider using clip-on lavaliere mics for interviews. Hide them on sets to capture actors.

- Use a directional mic on a fishpole boom for dramatic scenes or when a lav won't work.

- Always capture some room tone at every location. Use it in post to smooth voice edits.

- Layer your soundscape by adding sound effects, background sounds, and music in post-production.

- Keep sound "families" on their own tracks, that is, don't mix dialog and sound effects on the same track. Use different tracks and checkerboard sounds across the Timeline.

- Balance the elements in a mix to make speech intelligibility the number one priority.

- Find a place for everything in the mix and use contrast, dynamics, and fill the frequency spectrum.

Chapter 8

A Potpourri of Stylin' FX

Looking for some eye candy to entertain, motivate, and inform your audiences?
This grab bag of techniques should get your creative energy flowing.

Fast, Slow, Reverse, Strobe, and Ghost

Remember to use Ctrl+dragging and trimming events to slow down and speed up video. With Vegas, use velocity envelopes, too. However, there is one more method. Right-click an event and choose Properties. Adjust the playback rate. Higher numbers speed up and lower numbers slow down the video.

Movie Studio Users: Click the Event FX button>General tab to adjust playback rate.

To reverse an event in Vegas, right-click and choose Reverse.

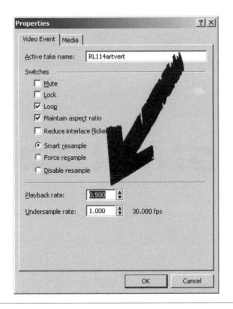

Assign a different frame rate to the selected event by adjusting the Under-sample rate in Event Properties. This can create some unusual strobing effects somewhat similar to that seen in *Band of Brothers*.

Right-click a track header and choose Duplicate Track from the pop-up menu to quickly make a copy.

Duplicate an event and place it on a track directly above itself. Apply undersampling to the bottom event. Adjust the opacity (40 to 60 percent) of the upper event to blend. This can create a dreamy quality to the video. For a different look, apply the Black and White FX to the bottom track, too.

Movie Studio Users: Event reverse and undersampling are not available.

Try different Vegas Compositing modes in conjunction with these effects.

Instead of undersampling, use Event Pan/Crop to either zoom in or out slightly on the top event. Adjust its opacity to blend with the unzoomed copy below. For more unique looks, add a motion blur only to the Pan/Cropped track.

Black and White/Old Film Looks

Select the Video FX tab in the Window Docking area and navigate to Black and White. Drag and drop one of the presets to a video track or event for the grayscale look.

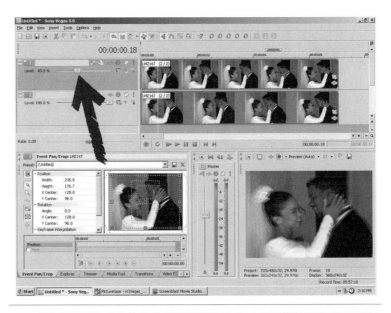

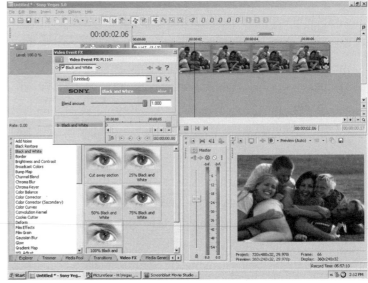

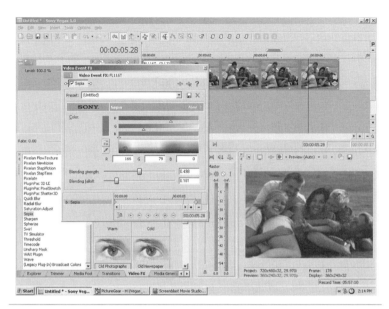

To gradually fade the effect in or out, use keyframing. Navigate to the first keyframe and adjust to taste. Place a keyframe at the end, and choose the effect's look.

For an old film look, use the Film Effects Video FX. Place the effect on either a track or event (or the entire project). Adjust the properties for the effect you want.

The Sepia Video FX simulates old photos, video, home movies, or a nostalgic look.

Add the Glow FX preset White Soft Glow and reduce Intensity to 1.8 for a unique spin on the old movie theme. Glow can impart a dreamlike, flashback, or romantic look, too.

Quick flashes of light can enhance the old movie look. Split an event in two by positioning the cursor and pressing S on the keyboard. Turn on automatic crossfades by clicking the Toolbar icon or using Ctrl+Shift+X.

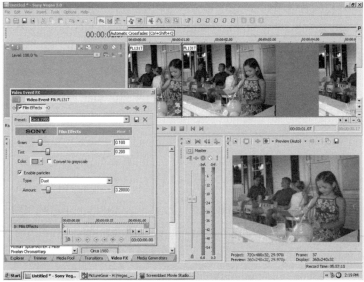

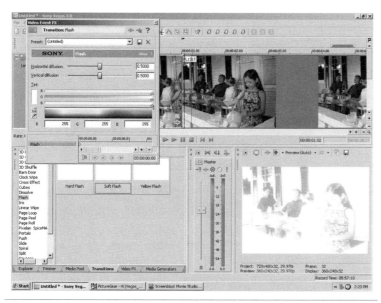

Overlap the split events slightly and drag the Flash transition Soft Flash preset from the Transitions tab of the window docking area to the crossfade.

Movie Studio Users: There is no Flash transition available. Insert a few frames of solid color white between events instead.

Use the Flash transition to simulate taking pictures. Add the appropriate sound effect to complete the illusion.

Night Vision and Turn Day into Night

Simulate the look of night-vision goggles. Use the Gradient Map Night Vision preset and add the Glow FX White Highlights preset followed by Film Grain FX Subtle preset. Drop down the opacity a little to darken the image.

Movie Studio Users: Simulate the look with Color Balance and Glow as neither Gradient Map nor Film Grain are available.

For a day-for-night simulation, add both the Color Balance and Brightness and Contrast Video FX to the track or event.

Set the Color Balance Blue to 0.200 and check the Highlights button.

Set the Brightness and Contrast to Brightness –0.25, Contrast to 0.35, and Contrast Center to .5. Adjust these sliders for the look.

Shoot when shadows are long (early morning or late afternoon) and avoid showing the sky when simulating day-for-night on location.

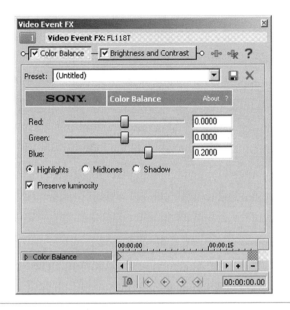

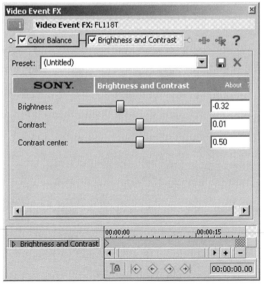

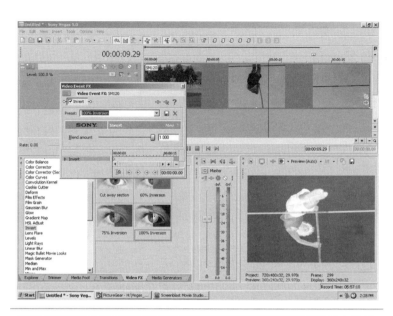

Unique Color and Shape Effects

Invert Video FX turns your video into a film negative. Blend amount balances the effect.

The Threshold Video FX yields a posterized look. Combine it with the Black and White filter for more creative options.

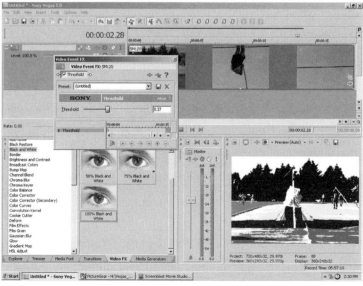

Simulate an oil painting look—especially on stills—using the Min and Max Video FX. Check Minimum and Circular area processing and set the Horizontal range to 0.110 and Vertical range to 0.068.

Preview before and after applying FX in Vegas by engaging Split Screen View in the Preview Window.

Distort the video using Pinch/Punch, Spherize, Swirl, or Wave. Drag the filter to the track or event and go through the presets for some instant effects. Animate these effects using keyframes for unique ideas.

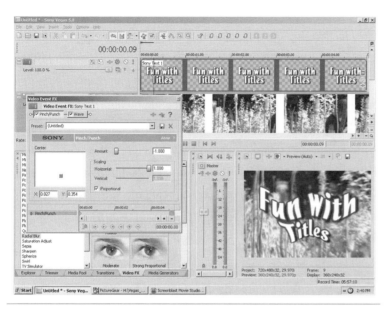

These unusual effects are ideal for dressing up titles and simulating 3D looks.

Create two different title events and add the Wave Video FX to both.

Tip: Need some inspiration? Watch Entertainment Tonight, Access Hollywood, or any music video channel. Emulate what you see with your projects.

Select the first title event and set its first keyframe to the Cut Away Section preset. Add the end keyframe and choose the Small preset.

Substitute the Swirl Video FX for a different title look.

Select the second title event and set its first keyframe to the Small preset and its end keyframe to the Cut Away Section preset. Crossfade the two events and preview as one title wiggles to unreadable then the second title wiggles to full readability.

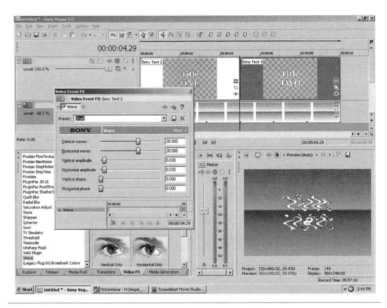

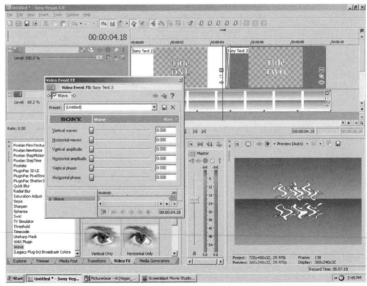

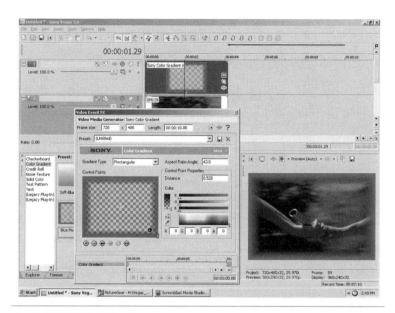

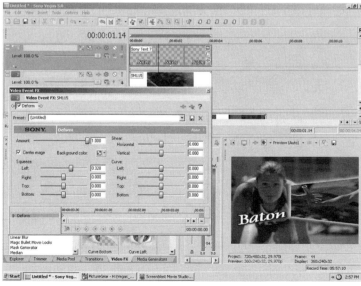

Borders, Widescreen, and Letterboxing

Place a border around the video by dragging the Border Translucent Blue Border preset to a video event or track. Adjust the color and opacity of the border as needed.

Tip: Use the Border FX coupled to track motion in Vegas to place frames around picture-in-picture effects.

Simulate 3D looks using the Deform Video FX. First, use track motion in Vegas and create a picture-in-picture (PIP) look. Drop the Deform plug-in on the event or track. Start with the Squeeze Left preset and adjust the Squeeze Left slider to 0.300 for a simulated look. Work with the Shear sliders (try –0.3H and 0.25V) to perfect the effect.

Movie Studio Users: Create PIP effects using Event Pan/Crop.

Turn your project into the 16×9 wide-screen format. Click File\>Properties and choose and the NTSC DV Wide-screen template from the drop-down list.

Right-click the Preview window and choose Simulate Device Aspect Ratio to better gauge the look.

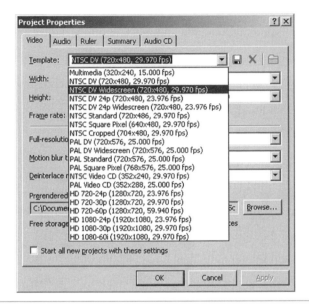

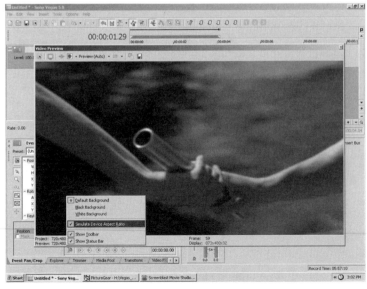

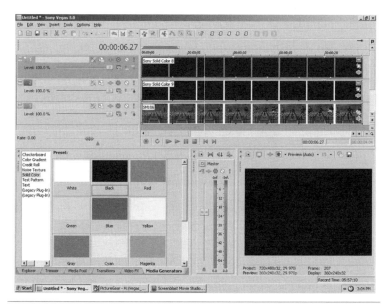

Create a fake letterbox effect, too. Create two new video tracks and make sure they are at the top of the project. Insert the Solid Color Black preset from the Media Generators tab on each track. Extend them both for the entire length of the project.

Use Event Pan/Crop to match the widescreen aspect ratio.

In Event Pan/Crop for the top event, enter 640 in its Y Center. This places a black band at the top of the screen.

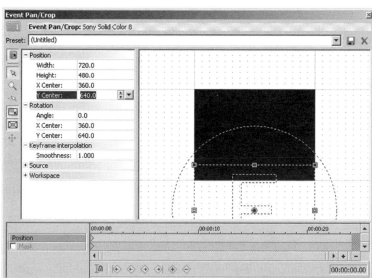

Set Event Pan/Crop for the bottom event to –160 for its Y Center. This is the black band for the bottom.

For smaller letterboxing use 680 and –200 instead.

Add Pizzazz to Titles

Wish your titles would do something more? Drag and drop the Lens Flare Sunburst Effect preset from the Video FX tab of the window docking area to a title event.

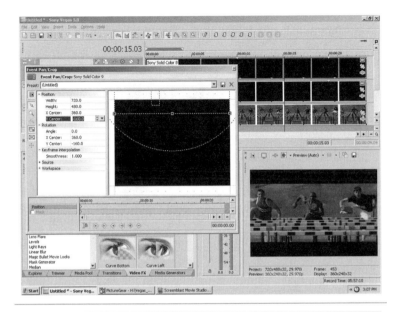

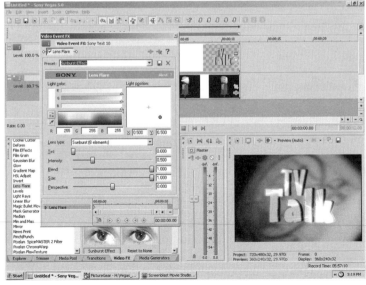

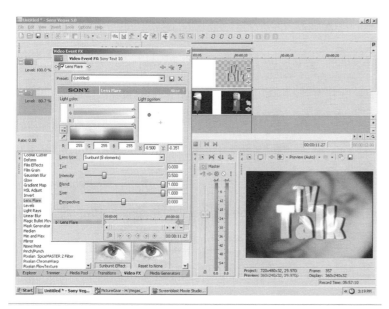

Leave the preset parameters for the first keyframe. Place a new keyframe at the end. Click and drag the brown circle in the Light Position box from the lower right to the upper left. Preview how the lens flare moves across the title.

Use the Light Rays filter in a similar way. Add a title event and fade it in. Add the Cyan Spotlight preset to the title.

Add additional keyframes in Vegas and keep moving the light around in a circle or back and forth to add extra interest to a static title.

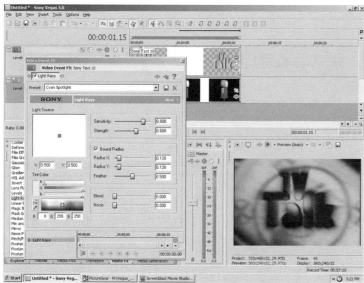

Add a keyframe about midway and select the Sparkling Light Rays preset from the drop-down list.

Move a little further along the keyframe Timeline and add another keyframe, choosing Reset to None. Preview the results.

Movie Studio Users: Start with the effect full on and then set to no effect for the End keyframe to recreate this effect.

For more title animation, add Tracking and Leading keyframes to the text event. You might also try inserting a transition to a fade in or out on a title.

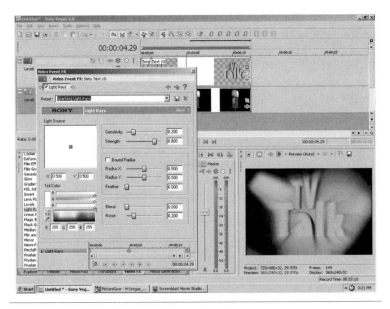

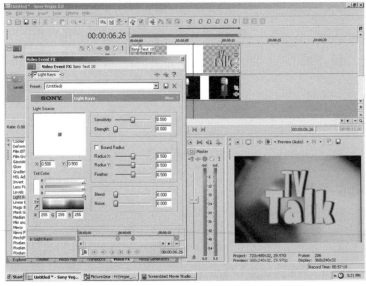

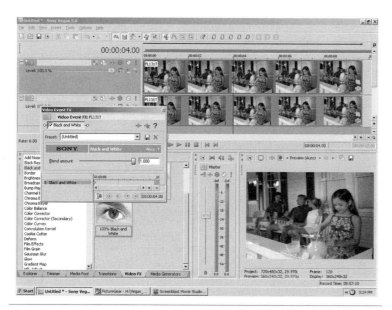

Cookie Cutter Cool

Place the same event on two adjacent video tracks. Drag and drop the 100 percent Black and White preset from the Black and White Video FX on the bottom event. Alternately, substitute Gaussian blur (or another filter) for the B/W FX.

Add the Cookie Cutter Video FX Picture-in-Picture preset to the top video event.

Adjust the position as needed. Color shows through where the box is while the rest of the video is B/W. Animate the box using keyframes to follow action.

While the cookie cutter works fine for mixing color and B/W as described above, it won't simulate the color people in a black and white world popularized by the film *Pleasantville*. This effect requires Vegas and some specific shooting techniques. First, lock down the camera on a tripod and shoot the scene without anything happening in it (no camera moves either). Shoot the scene a second time with some action in it, say an actor in view talking. Bring both clips to Vegas and place them on two tracks, one above the other. Add the B/W Video FX to the bottom track. Change the compositing mode on the top track to "Difference squared."

The "Cops" effect

Need to hide an identity, license plate, product, body part, gesture, or other material? Place the same event on two adjacent video tracks, one on top of the other. Add the Large Pixelate preset to the bottom event.

Add the cookie cutter Circle, Center preset to the top event. Change the Method to "Cut away section" by choosing from the drop-down list.

Position the circle, resize, and feather as needed. Use keyframes to follow the action. Also, animate the Pixelate filter to obscure more detail.

Substitute Gaussian Blur for the Pixelate FX for a subtler result.

Extremely Quick Slideshow Production

Need to create a slideshow from a bunch of stills fast? Click Options>Preferences>Editing and set "New still image length (seconds) to the duration you want for each slide (four or five is good).

Check "Automatically overlap multiple selected media when added" Under the Cut-to-overlap conversion, enter 1.250 as the Amount (seconds) value.

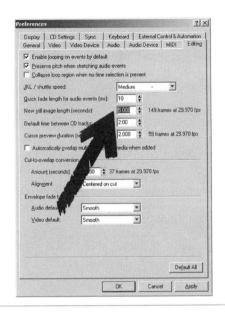

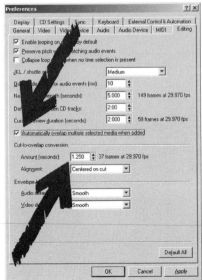

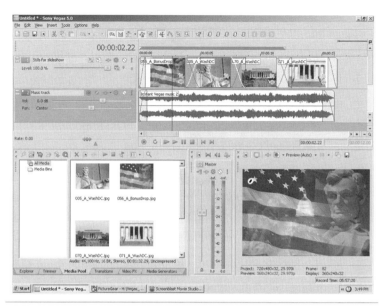

Create a new track on the Timeline. Select all your images using Explorer or the Media Pool and drag them to the track. Add some music and you're finished!

Rotate or adjust the aspect ratio on some stills as needed.

Export a Still from the Timeline

This process exports a high-quality, deinterlaced still from Vegas. Position the cursor at the frame to export. Set the Preview window to Best, Full.

Use the VASST Ultimate Script to export a sequence of stills from your video project.

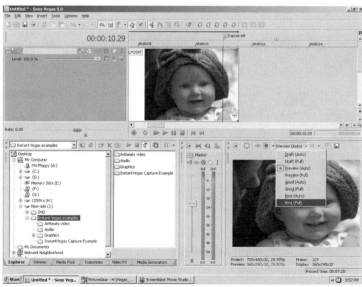

Go to File>Properties>Video tab.

- Change Field order to None (progressive scan).

Make sure you set the File Properties back to the previous setting after grabbing stills.

- Full-resolution rendering quality to Best.

- Deinterlace method to Interpolate fields.

- Click OK.

Click the Copy Snapshot to Clipboard button. Switch to a graphics program and paste it.

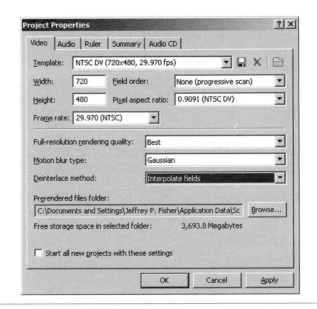

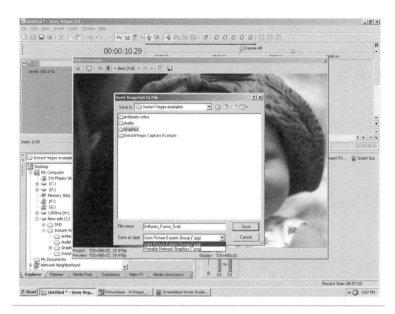

Or click the Save Snapshot to File button. Choose the file format (JPG or PNG) and a storage location using the dialog box that displays.

Note: The following section applies to Vegas only.

Vegas Bezier Masking

While the cookie cutter is a handy tool, Bezier masking is even more versatile. Find it in the Event Pan/Crop dialog. Click the check box to engage the mask and reveal its tools. Top to bottom they are:

- Show/Hide Properties

- Normal Edit Tool

- Anchor Creation Tool

- Anchor Deletion Tool

- Split Tangent Tool

- Zoom Edit

- Enable Snapping

- Move Freely (or restrict movement)

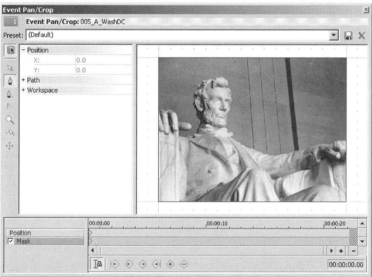

Click the Anchor Creation Tool and draw a mask by clicking on the image. This inserts a point.

Add another anchor point and notice the line connecting the two points.

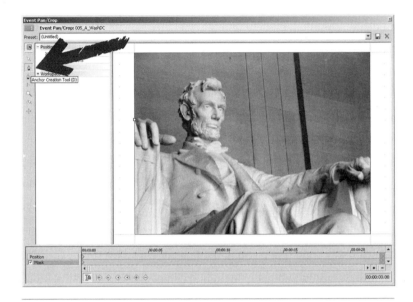

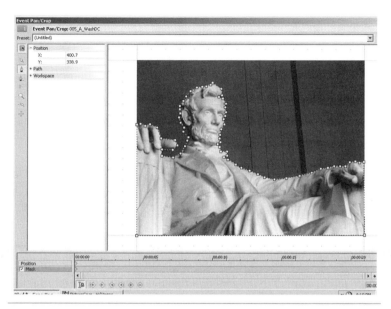

Continue adding points as needed. Make sure you connect the last anchor to the first to complete the mask.

Switch to the Split Tangent Tool and click an anchor point. Click and drag to fine-tune the curves.

Zooming in can make it easier to place anchor points more accurately.

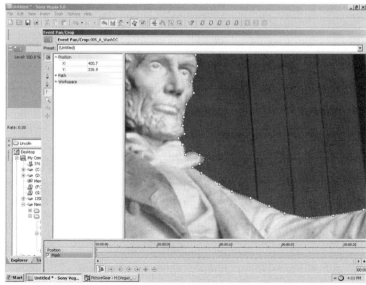

Options under Path properties provide further control over the mask.

Obviously, Bezier masks can be animated over time. For example, you could trace an actor and create a frame-by-frame mask and then composite him in another place.

Events can have multiple Bezier masks.

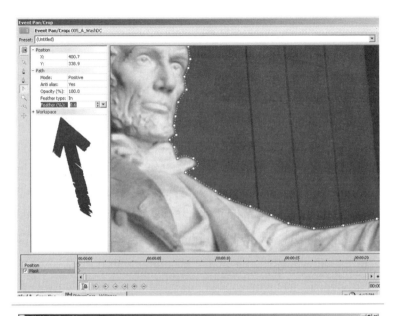

One clever Vegas user created an animation using Bezier masking to create and animate characters. (Courtesy of Mike Chenoweth.)

Freeze-Frame Foreground with Changing Background

A popular effect freezes a person in a scene and replaces the background. Create two video tracks and place the action scene on the top and the new background below it.

Tip: For a superpowerful example of Bezier masking and cartoon creation, check out the chenopup-mountain.veg from the www.vasst.com/login.htm site.

Locate the stop action point and place a velocity filter on the track, setting it to zero (0) at the desired position. Ignore this step if you are using a still. Leave the cursor at that point.

Open the Event Pan/Crop dialog box. Turn on the Sync Cursor and engage the Bezier mask. Place a keyframe that corresponds to the freeze frame. Trace the actor to create the mask. When complete, the background shows through at that point.

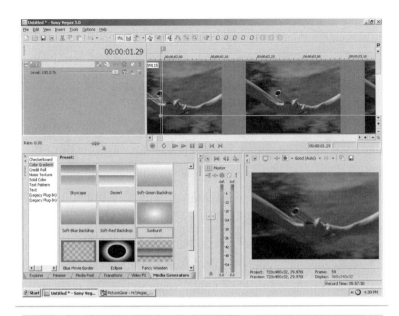

Place another keyframe just before the last and choose the Default option from the preset list. This ensures that the mask doesn't display until the right moment.

Use Track Motion to add shadow or glow to Bezier-masked events, too.

Adding Motion Blur

The powerful keyframing animation tools in Vegas lend themselves well to creating motion on titles, stills, and so forth. Adding some blur to these elements can make them more convincing. Or you could use motion blur as another trick up your proverbial sleeve.

Motion blur is global to the project. Add it on the master video output bus. Click View>Video Bus Track or use the Ctrl+Shift+B shortcut.

Right-click in the Video bus and choose Insert/Remove Envelope>Motion Blur Amount. This inserts a purple envelope line along the bottom of the video bus. Add points and shape the envelope. Preview the look and adjust to taste.

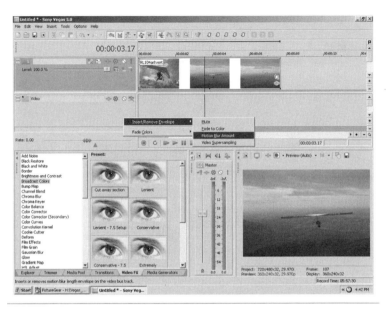

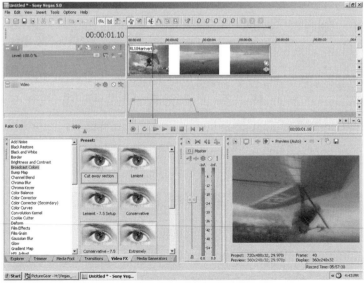

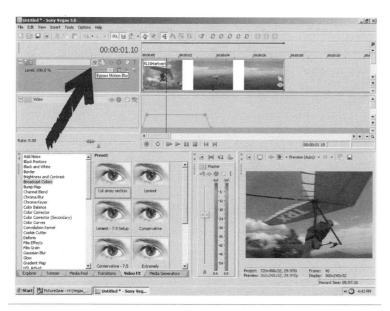

Since motion blur is global, each video track has a Bypass Motion Blur button. Engage the button to keep motion blur from being applied to events on that track. For example, apply motion blur to a zooming title, but not the background it "flies" over.

Motion blur reduces real-time playback significantly. Do a quick RAM render (Shift+B) to preview the project at the full frame rate.

3D Transitions

Vegas includes several 3D transitions. Drag and drop them from the Transitions tab of the Window docking area to an event fade-in or fade-out or the crossfade between two events.

Use the Cross Effect and Zoom transitions along with 3D track motion (see below) for more variety.

3D Track Motion

Track motion goes far beyond simple picture-in-picture effects. Vegas includes a 3D mode for positioning PIPs, titles, and more. Click the Track Motion button on a video track header. Access the composite modes in the upper-left corner. Choose 3D Source Alpha from the drop-down list.

The dialog box provides control over the X, Y, and Z positioning of the track along with the resizing capabilities in 2D track motion. There are several layout choices by clicking the Layout drop-down list. Switches along the top include:

- Toggle snapping on and off

- Edit in object space

- Prevent movement X, Y, or Z

- Lock aspect ratio

- Scale about center

- Prevent scaling for X, Y, or Z

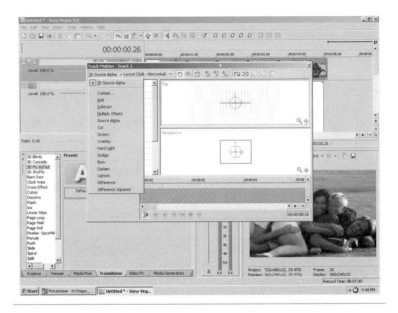

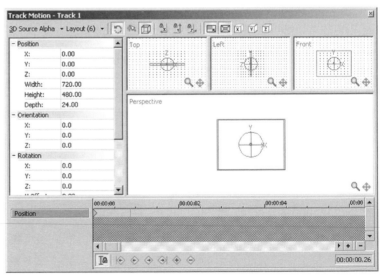

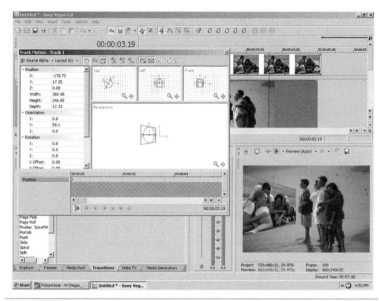

Manipulate the box and preview the results. Enter values in the Properties directly, too.

The real power comes from using keyframes to change the 3D track over time.

You can't add a shadow or glow to 3D track motion.

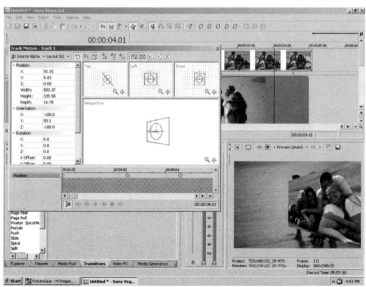

Click the Expand Track Keyframes button to see the track motion keyframes on the Timeline. Click and drag to adjust timing. Right-click a keyframe and choose options from the pop-up menu.

Apply 3D Track Motion to multiple tracks for interesting results.

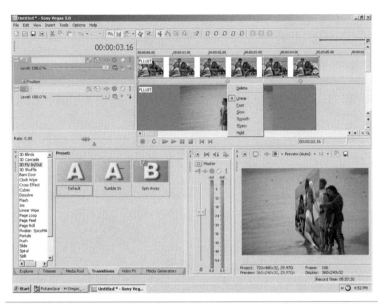

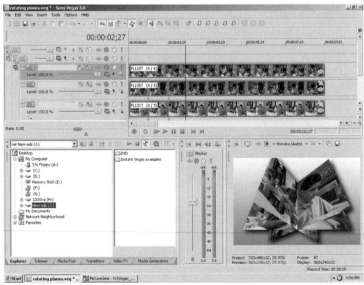

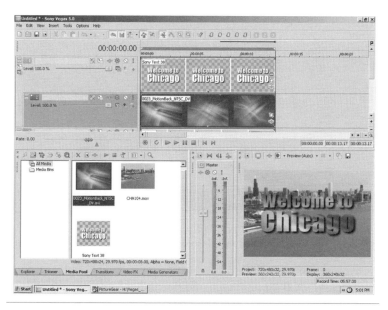

3-D Composites

Compositing in Vegas is incredibly robust! There is 3D Track Motion for composited tracks, too. This examples comprises a text event with video showing inside it. Set the top text event track's compositing mode to Multiply (Mask). Add some motion video to the track directly below and click its Make Compositing Child button.

Click the Parent Composite mode and choose 3D Source Alpha.

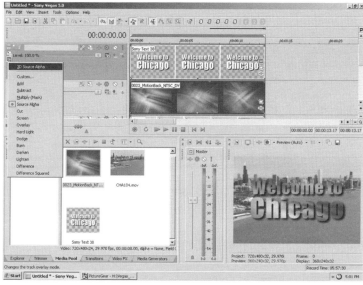

Use the dialog box to manipulate the composited tracks as one unit in 3D space.

Add a track above the first two. Click the Make Parenting Child in the second track.

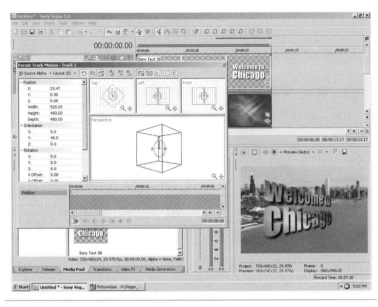

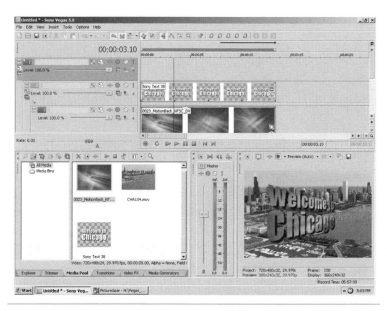

Click the Make Parenting Child in the third track to maintain the proper nesting relationship.

Open the top track's Parent Motion dialog and add a shadow. Preview how there is motion video in the text, positioned together in 3D space, with a shadow, too.

Parent tracks control the compositing effects of lower child tracks.

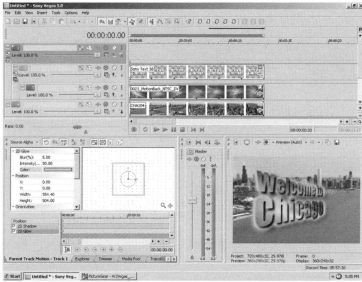

In this example, three independent tracks (tracks 3, 4, and 5) move with 3D motion. They are all compositing children of a single parent (track 2) with 3D motion applied. This controls the 3D motion of the group. The top parent (track 1) applies shadow only to the parts.

Note that 3D composites may create lengthy render times.

Nest tracks in various parent-child relationships to create some eye-popping results.

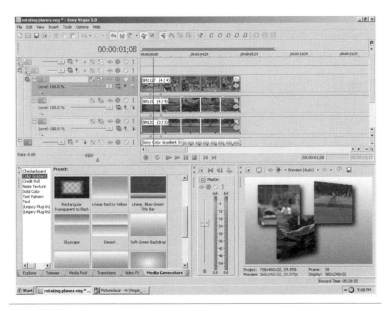

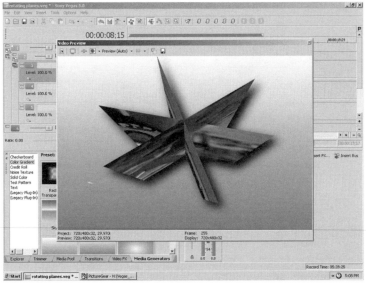

Chapter 9

Show Your Stuff

You've labored over your audio and video, and now it's time to deliver your latest masterpiece to the world. This chapter features tips for printing back to DV tape, rendering to a variety of formats, including DVD, and preparing for web streaming.

External Preview

Vegas allows preview of the Timeline on an external monitor. Connect a FireWire device such as a camcorder to the computer and also connect its analog out to a standard TV.

Movie Studio Users: Vegas Movie Studio does not support external preview to a television or broadcast monitor.

Set the Preview to Preview (Full).

Click the Preview on External Monitor button and play the Timeline. The video shows on the monitor.

If you see (Frame Recompressed), the video is not DV and may not have the same quality as DV played from the Timeline on an external monitor. Be sure that Recompress Edited Frames is checked in the Options>Preferences> Video Editing dialog. Otherwise, playback of edited media could be affected.

Several commercial DVDs, such as Pirates of the Caribbean, have audio and video setup tools that you can use to tweak your playback system. You can also purchase calibration DVDs, but you'll find the home theatre setup discs to be just as good for a quarter the cost.

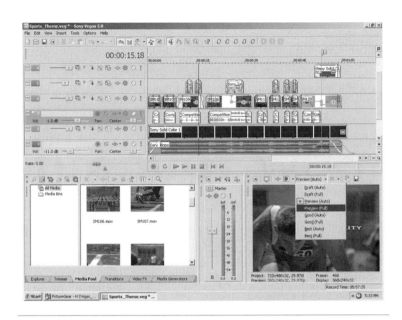

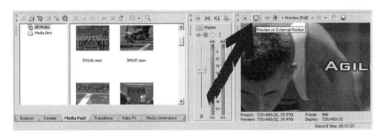

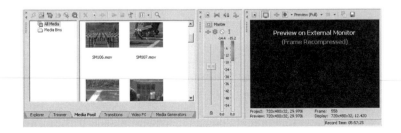

Why Render?

As we pointed out earlier, both Vegas and Vegas Movie Studio use project files, keeping the media separate. Therefore, to distribute the finished product, all the individual components—video, stills, titles, graphics, and sound—need to be rendered or compiled together as one finished video file. Rendering is akin to baking a cake where all the ingredients are cooked into one final product after blending or mixing.

Rendering is a non-real-time process, sometimes faster but more often significantly slower than the project's final length. Render times are project- and hardware-dependent. The more complex the video, such as one with many transitions, FX, and mixed media types, the longer it takes to render. The faster the computer, the quicker the render time. For example, it may take a few seconds to render a five-minute audio-only piece and several hours to render a one-minute video.

The rendering process is the same whether your final output is destined for tape, DVD, or the web. Only the particular file formats change.

- DV—render to the same DV codec as the camcorder using the AVI format.

- DVD—render to MPEG-2, the standard format for DVDs.

- Print to tape (PTT)—render and copy the file to tape using the DV format (see above).

- Quicktime—render to the Apple-supported format. Use Quicktime/TGA format to export to third-party apps for compositing.

- SVCD—render to MPEG-2 with lower resolution than DVD and deliver on CD-R.

- Uncompressed—render to full resolution, 4:4:4 video using the AVI format. These files are huge and will not play in real time. They're useful for archiving or when upsampling to HD.

- VCD—render to MPEG-1 and deliver on a CD-R. Many DVD players can play VCDs which hold up to 60 minutes of video that is near-VHS quality. Bitrate is 1.5 Mbps, so they're not suitable for high-quality video.

- Web—render to Web streaming formats such as Real Media, Windows Media, and Quicktime. Use this to render to Windows Media High Definition.

- YUV—render to a compressed, 4:2:2 lossless format smaller than uncompressed video and also suitable for archiving and upscaling and upsampling.

Make the render the only computing task (close programs, stop surfing the Net, etc.) to decrease render times.

Movie Studio Users: Click the Make Movie icon in the Toolbar or File>Make Movie to access the Make Movie—Select Destination dialog box. There are several choices:

- Save it to your hard drive—renders to a variety of formats to the hard drive location of your choice.

- Burn it to DVD—launches Sonic MyDVD for authoring and encoding.

- Burn it to Video CD (VCD) or CD-ROM—renders and copies the files to a standard CD-R.

- Publish it to the Web—renders to a variety of web-based streaming formats.

- Save it to Sony devices—renders and places the file on the Sony device of your choice.

- Save it to your camcorder's DV tape—renders and then prints to tape (just the opposite of capture).

- E-mail it—renders to smaller, lower-quality files for sending as e-mail attachments.

- Create an HTML page that includes it—renders to a web format and creates the page so others can access the video.

Refer to sections below for specific tips.

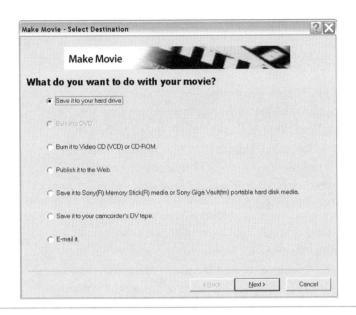

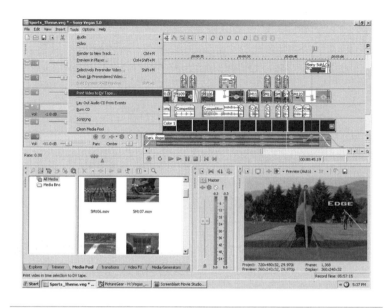

Print to Tape (PTT)

Connect your DV camcorder as if you are capturing footage. Make sure you insert either a blank DV tape or navigate to the point where you wish to record the file.

To print to DV tape directly from the Timeline, choose Tools>Print Video to DV Tape.

If any video is not already in the DV format, it will need to be pre-rendered before the PTT will continue. If that is only a few titles, transitions, and so forth, this is no big deal. The render will be fast and the PTT successful.

However, if your project is highly complex, render the file to the hard drive BEFORE using PTT (see below).

Movie Studio Users: Files are always rendered completely before PTT. We recommend using the Make Movie> Save it to your hard drive option first and choosing the NTSC DV template.

When that operation completes, use the Make Movie>Save it to your camcorder's DV tape option. Check Use an Existing File and enter the file name and path.

To print to tape from an existing file, launch Video capture through File> Capture Video or click the Capture Video button in the Media Pool. Navigate to the Print to Tape tab.

Click the Add Files button and choose the files to PTT.

PTT will overwrite any existing video on a tape. Use a blank tape or cue the camcorder to the proper place on an existing tape. You can also specify a particular start time on the tape in the PTT dialog. Just be sure the tape has timecode on it prior to starting the render.

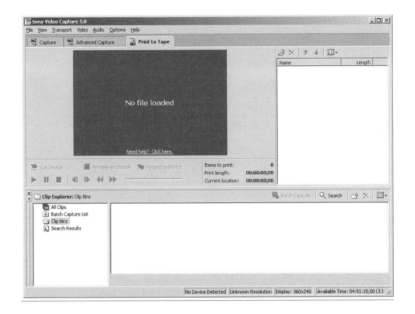

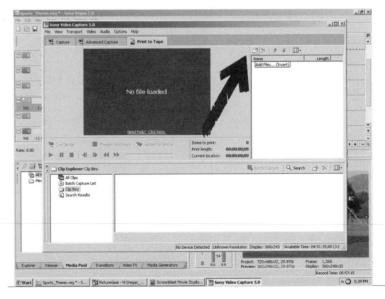

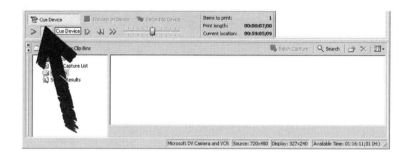

Cue the camcorder to the proper place on the tape and click the Record to Device button.

Mind the warning dialog and click Yes to continue the PTT.

The operation stops automatically when the files end or when manually ended.

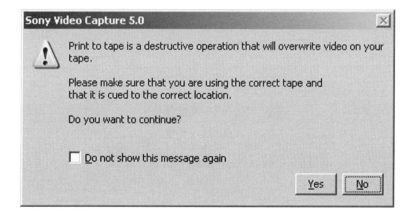

Movie Studio Users: From the PTT tab of the Capture dialog, choose File> Open and select the video file to PTT. Cue the camcorder then click the Record to Device button. The warning dialog reminds you that you tape should be blank or properly cued. Click Yes to continue and the PTT begins.

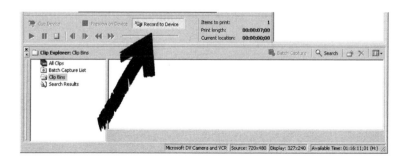

Render to a DV File on the Hard Drive

Click File>Render As to display the dialog box. From the Save As type drop-down list choose Video for Windows (*.avi).

From the Template drop-down list, choose NTSC DV. This is the same DV format as your camcorder.

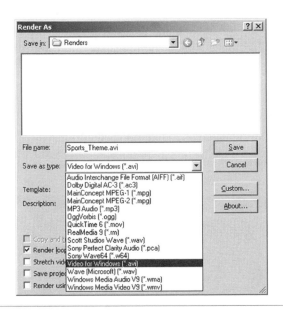

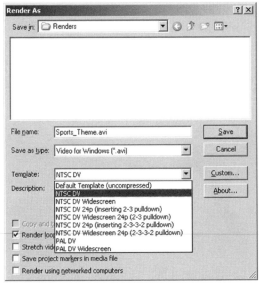

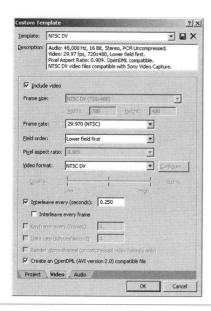

Click the Custom tab on the Render As dialog for more options. Typically, the default settings are ideal for the DV render.

Name the file, navigate to a location on your hard drive to store it, and then press Save to start the render process.

Substitute the PAL DV Template if it applies.

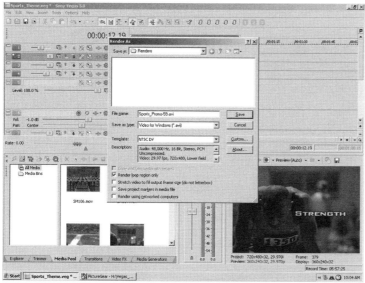

The dialog box indicates the render progress.

Render time indicated may not always be a true indicator of render time remaining, depending on the type of processing left in the project.

Movie Studio Users: Use Make Movie>Save it to your hard drive option and choose the Video for Windows (*.avi) format>NTSC DV template.

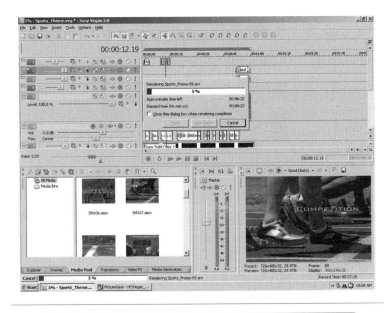

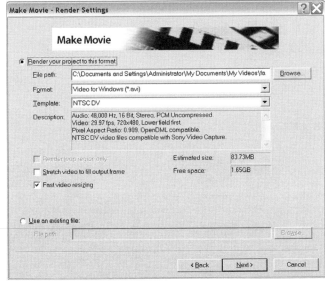

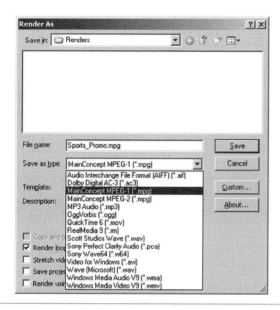

Render to VCD (MPEG-1)

It is possible to burn a VCD from the Timeline, but again, rendering the file first and then burning from the completed file is a less problematic workflow.

Click File>Render As to display the dialog box. From the "Save as type" drop-down list choose MainConcept MPEG-1 (*.mpg).

From the Template drop-down list, choose VCD NTSC (or PAL).

When the render completes, insert a blank CD-R into your CD burner. Choose Tools>Burn CD>Video CD. Check Use an existing file and Browse to the file created in the earlier step. Click OK to burn the VCD.

Movie Studio Users: Click Make Movie>Burn it to Video CD (VCD) or CD-ROM. The software renders the file first, then makes the disc.

MPEG-2 Encoding Tips

The nature of MPEG-2 encoding means that getting a quality output requires a little more work on your part. There is often video noise along the outer screen edge. The encoder allocates resources to this junk. Eliminate the noise and the encoder concentrates on your hard work instead. Also, reducing the color information results in a better encode.

Before rendering, prepare your video in two ways. One, crop the video slightly using Event Pan/Crop. Come in about six pixels from the edge—714x476 with aspect ratio turned on.

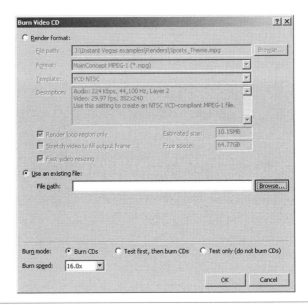

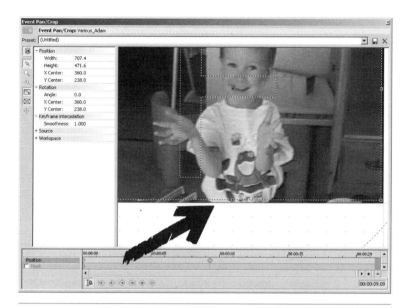

If the source was analog tape, such as VHS, crop to eliminate the analog banding noise along the bottom.

Two, reduce the color saturation by 10 to 15 percent. Drop the HSL Adjust Video FX on the Preview window and set the saturation slider to between 0.85 and 0.90. This reduces the color slightly but ultimately makes the final MPEG-2 look better.

Cropping and reducing saturation make web encodes look better, too.

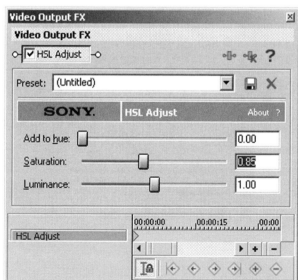

Render to DVD (MPEG-2)

DVDs must be authored separately, but you can render your file to the proper MPEG-2 format from Vegas. Click File> Render As to display the dialog box. From the "Save as type" drop-down list choose MainConcept MPEG-2 (*.mpg).

From the Template drop-down list, choose DVD NTSC (or PAL).

Drop the Black Restore filter onto the project. Set this to the Streaming preset. This will remove some of the black gradients in the project that will confuse the encoding process. This is good for any compressed media such as streaming formats, MPEG-1, or MPEG-2.

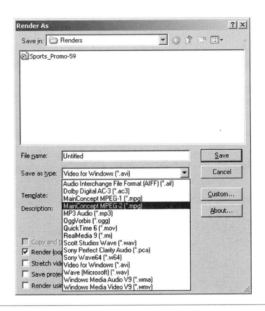

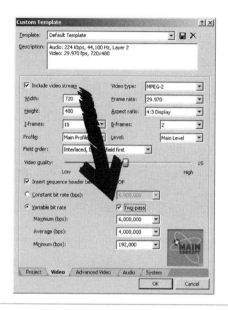

Click the Custom button and navigate to the Video tab. Check the Two-pass option and Vegas will go through the file twice, resulting in a higher-quality encode.

Two-pass encoding doubles the render time.

There are many MPEG-2 customization options that are far beyond the scope of this book. Use the dialog's Help button (?) for pop-up explanations of parameters. Experiment with different settings to see how they affect the output, too.

Click OK to close the Template dialog. Name the file, choose its location, and click Save to start the render.

Once the render completes, use DVD-A to author the final DVD. For more information on using this program, get the *Introductory DVD-Architect* DVD, also from VASST.

Movie Studio Users: Click Make Movie>Save it to your hard drive option and choose the MainConcept MPEG-2 (*.mpg) format>DVD NTSC template. There is no two-pass option. Author the DVD using the DVD Architect Studio software.

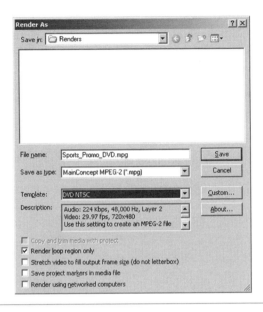

Render DVD Video and AC-3 Audio Separately

If you've purchased Vegas+DVD-A or the optional Dolby AC-3 plug-in, render your audio and video independently. Choose MainConcept MPEG-2 (*.mpg) format>DVD Architect NTSC video stream Template. This renders the video only ready for authoring in DVD-A.

When the video stream render completes, select the Dolby Digital AC-3 (*.ac3) format and choose the Stereo DVD Template (or 5.1 Surround DVD).

If you use the same name and location for the separate audio and video files, DVD-A will automatically keep them together when authoring.

Click the Custom button and set the Dialog normalization to −31dB from the drop-down list. Changing the normalization curve makes your AC-3 playback level identical to your project's audio level.

Navigate to the Preprocessing tab and set Dynamic range compression>Line mode profile to None.

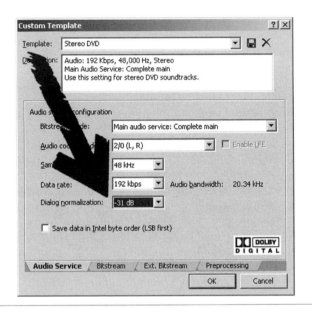

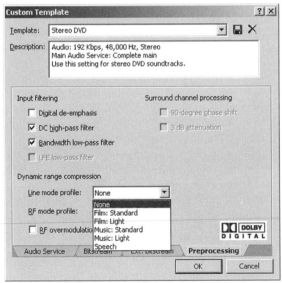

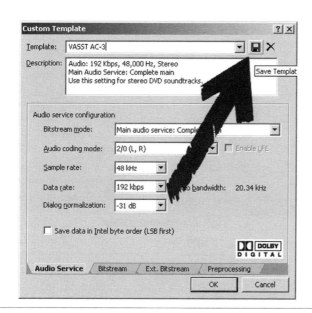

Give the Template a name (such as VASST AC-3) and click the Save Template button. Click OK to close the Custom dialog and then save to render the audio only to AC-3 ready for DVD-A.

The AC-3 Custom tab controls Dolby AC-3 metadata. See Instant Surround for more details.

Render for Web Streaming

From the Render As dialog, choose Windows Media Video (*.wmv) or any of the other web formats from the "Save as type" drop-down list.

Select the Template required from the drop-down list. Notice that the supplied templates mirror Internet connection speeds.

Movie Studio Users: Choose Make Movie>E-mail it for Web streaming formats.

Render audio only

To render audio to standard CD-quality, choose Wave (Microsoft) (*.wav) and use the 44,100Hz, 16-bit, Stereo, PCM Template.

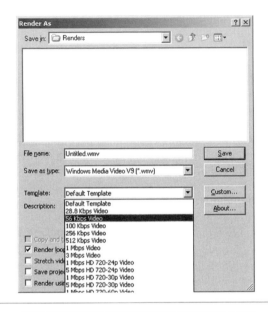

To render to MP3, choose MP3 Audio and select from the Templates. Typical MP3s use the 128Kbps or 160Kbps setting.

Using the Vegas Batch Render Script

Need to render to several different file formats from the same Vegas project Timeline? The included Batch Render script automates the tasks for you. Click Tools>Scripting>Batch Render.

Running scripts in Vegas requires the free Microsoft .NET framework installed.

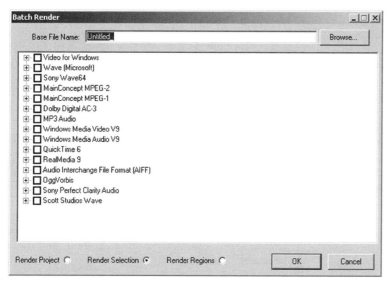

If you check a top-level choice, it will select and render *every* format under that heading. This is likely not what you'll want to do.

Instead, check only those file formats you need.

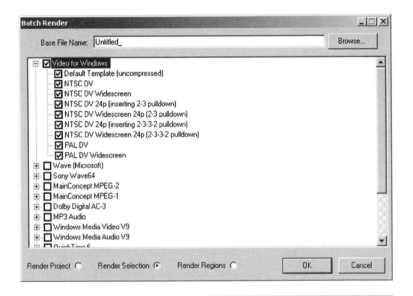

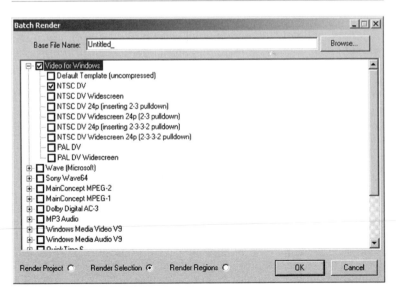

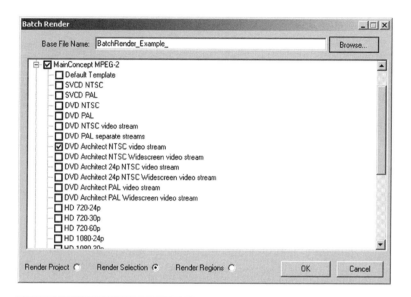

Enter a Base File Name and browse to the location to store the finished files. Click OK to start the render process. Be certain your hard drive has enough space to store the various rendered file types.

AC-3 is almost always a better choice than MPEG-1 audio, unless the known target audience only has very old equipment to play back the project. All computers less than four years old that contain DVD players will play back AC-3 files.

Archiving Projects

Storing your work for the future is a necessary workflow. Obviously, just saving the project file isn't enough, as you need to save the media, too. And it may be in many different places.

Sweep the Media Pool to clear any media that may be associated with the project, but not used in the final piece. Click the Remove All Unused Media from Project button.

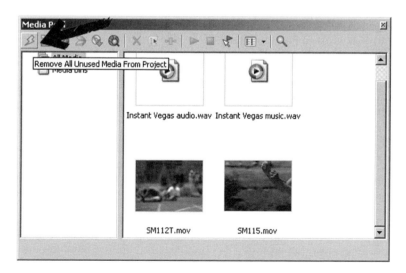

Click File>Save As and then check Copy and trim media with project.

Name the project and choose a storage location. Consider creating a new folder on a separate drive. Click OK.

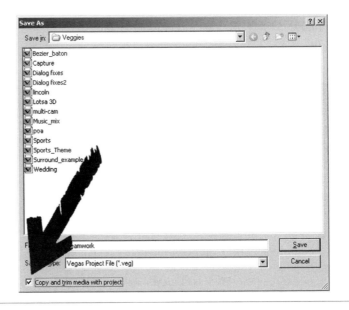

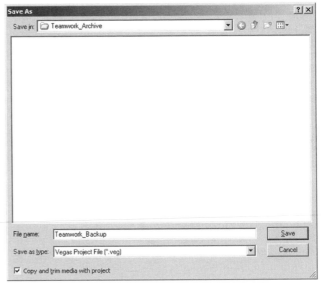

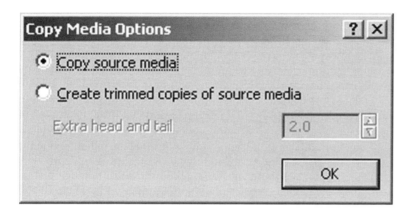

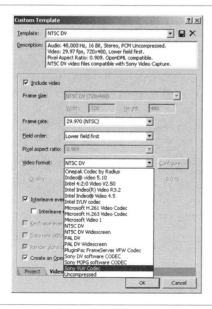

There are two options in the Copy Media Options dialog:

- Copy source media—copies all the media used in the project along with the project file to the specified location.

- Create trimmed copies of source material—copies the media in the project only as actually used with the option to include extra head and tail. For example, if you had a one-minute clip, but only used 10 seconds of it in the finished video, only 14 seconds of the clip would be copied (with a two-second head and tail). This leaves some handles should you need to re-edit.

Burn a data CD or DVD of archived projects as another backup!

Archiving Format

DV uses 4:1:1 color space, MPEG II uses 4:2:0, HDCam uses 4:2:2, and HD uses 4:4:4. Therefore, the ideal archiving format is uncompressed video. Another alternative is the Sony YUV codec which is 4:2:2 and creates smaller file sizes. It's great for re-rendering MPEG II files if necessary and upscales and upsamples well for moving content to the HD world.

Click File>Render As to display the dialog box. From the "Save as type" drop-down list choose Video for Windows (*.avi).

Choose the NTSC-DV or PAL-DV render template in almost all instances. There are other templates available for specialized use.

Render first to either Uncompressed or Sony YUV, then add this file to a new Vegas Timeline and render to MPEG-2 from it. Do this only if you need a source file for creating multiple formats. If rendering to print to tape only, or rendering to DVD only, render the project from the Timeline for optimum time savings.

Movie Studio Users: Choose Make Movie>Save it to your hard drive and choose the Video for Windows (*.avi) format and the Default Template (NTSC/PAL) Template.

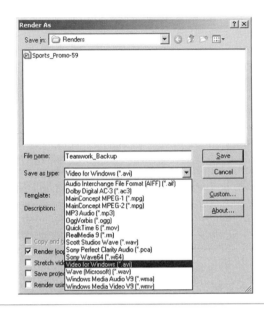

Chapter 10

Final Word

We hope you've learned a great deal about the Vegas and Vegas Movie Studio tools. And we hope you are excited to explore the creative possibilities with your work. Additional applications to learn after these are DVD Architect 2 and DVD Architect Studio. These will become the "icing" on your video cake, allowing you to distribute your masterpiece to whomever you wish. You can find specific DVDs on DVD Architect at the VASST site.

Questions?

If you need additional help with Vegas or Vegas Movie Studio (or general audio or video issues):

- Drop by the Vegas forum on Digital Media Net (www.dmnforums.com).

- Stop by the VASST Web site at www.vasst.com.

Contact Douglas at dse@sundancemediagroup.com and Jeffrey at jpf@jeffreypfisher.com. Although neither of us are tech support for the software, we'll try to respond as best we can. The forums mentioned above are usually the best places to seek technical answers, and questions are typically responded to within minutes of being asked on the DMN site. Plus, you can read questions from others, and learn much more in the process.

Additional Resources:

See the VASST DVDs, live training tour, and book pages on the www.vasst.com site, in addition to the free VEG files and tutorials found on the www.vasst.com/login.htm site.

You can also find a rather large selection of books related to digital audio and video on the www.cmpbooks.com web site. CMP Books is dedicated to bringing you great books without all the fluff found in many technical books.

Thanks for reading our write!

Jeffrey P. Fisher

Douglas Spotted Eagle

Want to sign up for e-mail updates for *Instant Vegas® 5?* Visit http://www.cmpbooks.com/maillist and select from the desired categories. You'll automatically be added to our preferred customer list for new product announcements, special offers, and related news.

Make Your Own Music Video

Ed Gaskell

Tune up, synch up, and lay down entertaining, professional-quality music videos. A music video pro tells all—from rehearsing the band and dealing with the egos to the nitty-gritty of synching video and audio tracks and compressing footage for streaming on the Internet.

4-Color softcover, 192 pp, ISBN 1-57820-258-2, $44.95

Designing DVD Menus

Michael Burns and George Cairns

Design DVD menus with that cool, professional edge. Begin by cutting through the jargon and technical issues; then analyze an array of projects to see how to use animation, picture-within-picture, background movie clips, and audio and imaging effects to create stunning titles, menu screens, transitions, and interactive features.

4-Color softcover, 192 pp, ISBN 1-57820-259-0, $44.95

Lighting for Digital Video & Television, Second Edition

John Jackman

A complete course in video and television lighting. Detailed illustrations and real-world examples demonstrate proper equipment use, safety issues, troubleshooting, and staging techniques. This new edition features a 16-page, 4-color insert and new chapters on low-budget set-ups and lighting for interviews.

Softcover, 256 pp, ISBN 1-57820-251-5, $39.95